Scandinavian World Cooking

BY SAS AND THE BEST CHEFS IN SCANDINAVIA

Production INTELLECTA & SAS. *Project Manager* EVA-KARIN DAHL. *Editors* LARS PEDER HEDBERG & ANNA MICHELSON. *Recipe Editor* INGER GRIMLUND. *Photography* LENNART DUREHED. *Art Director* JOHAN CARLSSON. *Graphics* EBBA SVENNUNG. *Assistant Project Managers* STEFAN BJURHOLM, HÅKAN OLSSON & ERIK STENVALL. *Assistant Editors* JONAS ANDERSSON & BENGT ÅKESSON. *Translation* CLARE JAMES. *Pre-press & Printing* DB GRAFISKA. *Typography* SAS BODONI. *Paper* SILVER-BLADE. ISBN 91-630-5357-8. © SCANDINAVIAN AIRLINES SYSTEM. ALL RIGHTS RESERVED. PRINTED IN SWEDEN 1997. *Jacket* SADDLE OF RABBIT WITH HERB STUFFING, SAFFRON STOCK AND GRILLED VEGETABLES BY NORRLANDS BAR & GRILL.

EVERY RECIPE SERVES FOUR UNLESS OTHERWISE INDICATED

Pure Traditions

Nowadays, gravlax — raw salmon, sugar-salted and spiced — is regarded as a supremely high-class gastronomic item. It features on the menus of New York's and Tokyo's most elegant restaurants, in the distinguished company of Iranian Oscietre caviar and French Belons oysters. But this was not always the case.

On the contrary, the history of the roots of Scandinavian cuisine is largely one of deprivation, poverty, thrift, hunger — and sometimes famine. Many of the best-known Scandinavian dishes and specialities originated as staple foods of the poor: this applies to pickled salt *matjes* herring, marinated salt Baltic herring *(inlagd strömming)* and *gravlax*. Herring *(sill)* was once the only source of protein for the masses, a gift from God that enabled people to survive yet another harsh winter.

In the peasant communities of bygone days, each family lived on what its members themselves produced in the vegetable patch or the village. The storerooms, which were filled with food in the autumn, had to feed many mouths over the year ahead. Owing to the great distances and sparse population in Norway and Sweden, in particular, trade was on a smaller scale than in the rest of Europe.

Thrift became a virtue, and discarding food was unthinkable. Everything had to be used. Leftovers from the meal served on Monday were stewed for dinner on Tuesday, and the last morsels were boiled for soup on the Wednesday.

'Bone-rattling soup' *(benskrammelsoppa)*, a hotch-potch of all remaining scraps from the Christmas table, is a good example of old-fashioned, 'economical' Scandinavian food. So, too, are all the dishes made of animal entrails, such as calf's pluck, i.e. lungs *(lungmos)*, blood-bread soup *(blodbrödsoppa)*, black soup *(svartsoppa)* from Skåne (with such ingredients as goose blood and dripping), Norwegian sausage hash *(hakkpølsen)* and so on.

Many of these old dishes are turning up again in Scandinavia these days as delicacies, after nearly a century's exile in the recesses of the collective conscience. Young restaurateurs, in particular, see in these old-time paupers' provisions a treasury of

*Roots, indeed.
Root vegetables are part
of the Scandinavian
pauper tradition. Today,
flavourful roots such as
turnip, scorzonera root and
Hamburg (turnip-rooted)
parsley are in favour.*

pristine Scandinavian gastronomy that must not be allowed to disappear. Today, many of these raw materials are difficult to obtain and, by the same token, far from cheap.

A culinary journey through Scandinavia soon reveals how nature and the climate in the various regions have affected the cuisine. Few give a thought to the immensity of Scandinavia — both Sweden and Norway stretch across more latitudes and climatic zones than any other country in Western Europe — and these varied conditions have resulted in diverse culinary traditions.

The harsh climate in northern Sweden and Norway has 'necessitated' such delicacies as soft whey-cheese *(messmör)*, crispbread, thin unleavened bread *(tunnbröd*, which is available in both soft and crisp forms*)* and *gravlax*. The reindeer herded by the Lapps, or Sami as they prefer to be called, and the elk, or moose – the majestic king of the northern forests – were important protein sources. The cloudberries of the wetlands and lingonberries of the forests provided indispensable vitamin C in a world where the summer was fleeting and scope for cultivation small.

Elsewhere in Scandinavia, too, the winter lasts between three and five months. To a high degree, it has been essential to save and preserve the gifts of summer. Many of the typical flavours are derived from the substances and techniques used to make the food keep longer.

Originally, *gravlax* was a sour dish, not entirely unlike the malodorous fermented Baltic herring *sur(strömming)* of our own day, which is eaten as a ritual by inhabitants of the province of Norrland (roughly the northern half of Sweden) every August. The huge catches of salmon *(lax)* taken from the rivers in the late spring were hard to keep in store, and salt was expensive. Some astute person hit on the idea of digging a deep pit *(grav)* and burying the fish in it. With just a pinch of salt, the fish did not putrefy: instead, it just fermented and turned sour. One could then dig up the salmon and subsist on it throughout the winter. This 'pit salmon' *(gravlax)* was for centuries an important staple of the northern Swedish peasants' diet.

Four centuries ago the cooks to the aristocracy discovered that, after treatment with salt, sugar and spices, salmon would undergo a process that removed its 'raw' fishy flavour, without the flesh fermenting. This meant that the sour smell and flavour were eliminated. This dish inherited the name of its time-honoured peasant forerunner.

In northern Sweden and Norway, flour-milling was feasible only in the spring and autumn, when the millstreams contained enough water. However, storing six months' supply of flour was impossible, so prompt baking of bread that would keep was essential. The solution was the thin, dry crispbread with its virtually unlimited shelf life. This explains why to this day more crispbread and *tunnbröd* are eaten in the northern parts of Scandinavia than in the south.

Only three per cent of Norway's area is suitable for arable farming. Instead, the people have had to depend on animal husbandry and fishing. And the Norwegians are, of course, the world's most proficient at preparing fish. Herring is eaten in many forms: fresh, dried, smoked, salted, pickled with spice — and even as soup *(sildegryn)*. Pickled, salted mountain salmon trout *(rakørret)*, garnished with sour cream and onion, is another typical Norwegian speciality.

In the coastal areas, where fish is the overwhelmingly predominant staple food, eating habits have been determined by which species are caught at particular times of year. Thus in January and February cod was eaten, while in the spring it was salmon, and in the summer spiny dogfish, ocean perch or redfish, ling, cod and halibut. Between September and November came the shoals of herring, and from October to Christmas it was time for the coalfish to throng the fishing waters and cooking pots.

Otherwise, lamb and mutton are typical of Norway. Sheep roam freely on the mountains all through the summer, and the meat takes on a fine flavour from the wild herbs they eat. Another contribution of the mountains is small game, such as ptarmigan and hare.

The further south in Scandinavia one goes, the more fertile the soil becomes. The inhabitants of Skåne (Sweden's southernmost province, formerly under Danish rule) and the Danes are famed for their passionate attitude towards food – partly a consequence of their more abundant supply of food, with fat pigs and tasty, nourishing vegetables raised on the rich soil. Geese from Skåne and ducks from Denmark are still renowned for their fine dripping, and roast pork *(flæskesteg)* is a prized, typically Danish speciality. Danish cuisine deviates quite widely from Norwegian and Swedish in other respects as well. Denmark has always been more integrated in European culture than its Scandinavian neighbours, and its superb position between the North Sea and the Baltic has also created a natural spring-board for trade. The Danes have made the most of this and, in particular, engaged in trade with the East Indies. Curry spices, which in Scandinavia are perceived as more Danish than Indian, are used both in herring and in mayonnaise.

Skåne is still the granary of Sweden, but in Denmark a large-scale shift from cereal to livestock production took place at the end of the 19th century. Dairy farming and the production of beef and pork still form the basis of the country's agriculture, and are important Danish export industries.

Denmark, Norway and Sweden are all among the world's major cheese producers, and many delectable Scandinavian cheese varieties are exported and have won prestigious awards around the world. Cheese manufacture, too, has ancient roots. The popular Swedish variety known as *Prästost* ('vicar's cheese') was made at vicarages back in the 17th century, when the vicar's salary was paid partly in kind.

On Norwegian farms, cheese has long been made from the milk of goats and cows that grazed on the cool mountain slopes, where fresh pasturage abounded. The strong, sweet Norwegian *Ekte Geitost*, made from pure goat's milk, is still a national favourite, but there are also slightly milder-flavoured cheeses made from blended goat's and cow's milk.

Nonetheless, the best-known Scandinavian cheeses are Danish. Few forget their first encounter with the powerful odours and overwhelming flavours of a mature *Havarti* or *Gamle Ole*.

Otherwise, the *smørrebrød* – 'buttered bread', i.e. Danish open sandwiches – is Denmark's most celebrated contribution to world gastronomy. A countless variety of these sophisticated canapés exist; the Ida

Scandinavia is known for its fish of outstandingly high quality – here, salmon, ocean perch and salmon trout.

Davidsen restaurant in Copenhagen has 178 different kinds on the menu. They are eaten in a strictly defined order: a herring and a roast-beef *smørrebrød* should never share the same plate; herring should always precede salmon; cheese and rolled veal sausage *(rullepølse)* should not be mixed, and so forth. And each open sandwich is washed down with a 'little one' – a schnapps, dram or tot of aquavit.

The fact is that the rituals involved in partaking of the *smørrebrød* are largely identical with those relating to the similarly world-famous Swedish 'sandwich table', the *smörgåsbord*. Both were modelled on the Russian tradition of starting a meal with a few salty *hors d'oeuvres* to accompany a few glasses of vodka. In the 18th century a growing number of dishes were added to the Swedish 'brännvin table' *(brännvin*, literally 'fiery wine', is Swedish aquavit), until it became a meal in itself. In the mid-19th century, the *smörgåsbord* began to assume the somewhat orgiastic proportions it retains to this day – a plethora of dishes, often fatty, to which one should help oneself in the correct order. A true Scandinavian never mixes fish and meat or cold and hot food on the same plate. One should make at least five visits to the table, helping oneself first to the various kinds of pickled herring, then to the salmon and other fish dishes, followed in turn by the cold and hot meat dishes and finally the desserts. And the drams of *brännvin* – here, the schnapps is known as a *nubbe* – are of course a must throughout the meal.

Norway, too, has its counterpart to the *smörgåsbord*, the *koldtbord* ('cold table'), which is somewhat lighter than the Swedish version.

The first person to write about food in Scandinavia was the Roman historian Cornelius Tacitus, in the century before Christ. In his history of the Germans, he writes of the Nordic peoples: 'Their diet is simple: wild fruits, freshly shot venison and sour milk. Without culinary art, they still their hunger.'

Much water has flowed under the bridge since then – and with it have come inspiration, raw produce, seasonings and spices from the outside world.

The Vikings, for example, brought oats, millet, peas and broad beans from their journeys to west and east. Medieval monks, as well as Christianity, brought knowledge of gardening and fruit growing.

When the copious natural resources of Scandinavia began to be discovered, southern Germans and Walloons came to develop the mining and metal industry, while northern German merchants provided the towns with a functioning market and administration. Words from Low German reveal the original homeland of many Nordic dishes: northern Germany.

Sweden's small pancakes *(plättar)* came from Russia, and 'quintessentially Swedish' dolmas *(kåldolmar)* from military campaigns in Turkey – with the difference that we in Sweden roll cabbage leaves round a mixture of mincemeat and rice instead of vine leaves, and serve lingonberry jam with it.

In the 18th century, French cuisine began to set the tone. Sautéing, braising and flaming became popular, and people began to drink coffee and cocoa. In the same century, the potato made its real entry into Scandinavia, where the soil proved excellently suited to this small, round, South American root vegetable. Thus the population gained a new, important reserve of vitamin C and carbohydrate during the winter half of the year. Previously, a variety of turnip had been the staple crop, especially in Sweden – hence its name, the 'swede'.

Potatoes have become something of a common denominator to Scandinavian cookery as a whole, and form part of most everyday dishes. In the early summer, new potatoes are a high prized early vegetable in Norway, Denmark and Sweden alike. The hysteria that surrounds the domestically grown early crop exceeds the cult surrounding *Beaujolais Nouveau*, and prices per kilo start in the same category as *foie gras*.

Today, we who live in Copenhagen, Oslo or Stockholm eat pizza, bibimbap and sushi like all other modern 'citizens of the world'. But at weekends and on feast days and festive occasions, we stick to our traditions.

With all due respect to modern cross-cooking, what would a sunlit Scandinavian summer evening be without pickled herring and new potatoes fragrant with dill, a tasty beer and an ice-cold schnapps?

Round the World
in 80 Recipes

THE WORLD IS A MELTING-POT, THEY SAY – and nowadays it definitely stands on our cooker. When SAS decided to replace its traditional inflight food with a contemporary multi-cultural concept – Scandinavian World Cooking – it was a move in line with the dominant, long-standing megatrend in Scandinavian cuisine.

We Scandinavians have borrowed freely from other cuisines throughout history, but in the past seven or eight years more actively than ever before. In this period, Scandinavia has witnessed a dramatic increase in culinary interest, and in the major cities restaurants have emerged that by no means lag behind those of any international metropolis.

The Scandinavian cooking scene today is sparkling, spirited and attractive to the young, creative elite. The level of proficiency is advanced, and innovation is at a premium. Domestic traditions are being explored with the same enthusiasm as raw materials and techniques from other cuisines are tried out. The supply of exotic raw produce has increased rapidly. Cooks are also searching our own forests and waters with new eyes, and re-evaluating the culinary uses of forgotten, neglected and once rejected fish, molluscs and amphibia.

Unprejudiced mixing is the order of the day: the known with the unknown, the indigenous with the exotic. Not all the results, of course, are pleasing; but many are excellent. Numerous Scandinavian staple raw materials seem to lend themselves superbly to international adventures. One is herring, perhaps the most Scandinavian of all foods. Back in the 19th century, herring was already being prepared with various exotic flavourings and spices: allspice, mustard, curry, ginger, cinnamon, cloves, sandalwood, capers and currants. Today, young culinary artists are serving it in chili and garlic marinades, or with a lime or orange sauce.

In the major towns, it is now quite easy to obtain both fresh chilis – habanero, jalapeño or poblano – and fresh oriental green herbs such as coriander, morning glory and lemon grass. These will probably soon be as firmly integrated into Scandinavian cuisine as potato and dill.

Salmon – one of many Scandinavian classics that have found new expressions in a multicultural context. Salmon carpaccio from Norrlands Bar & Grill.

Dill is the herb that is most closely associated with Scandinavia. Snipping it over the new potatoes at Midsummer is almost a ritual, and dill plays an equally important part in the time-honoured rites of August, when its large flowering heads impart a unique, rich flavour to the dark-red freshwater cray-fish. But the fact is that dill was originally imported from China.

Giving prominence to fine raw produce, with its natural flavours and pristine appearance (which spells a lighter hand at the cooker), and using more vegetables and less fat, and vegetable rather than animal fat — these are some of the watchwords of modern Scandinavian cuisine. They also make up one of the two main features of SAS's Scandinavian World Cooking. The other consists of the felicitous unions between Scandinavian raw materials and tra-ditions on the one hand and, on the other, the best that foreign and ethnic cuisines have to offer.

The modern version of cross-cooking has been a global phenomenon for 20 years. The word is an American one, while the British prefer the expression 'eclectic cooking', i.e. a mixture of styles — a concept derived from the world of architecture, where the ten-dency to combine stylistic elements from the rococo and neoclassicism, for example, is termed 'eclectic'.

CROSS-COOKING IS THUS NO NEW PHENOMENON. Global gastronomy has always developed by borrow-ing from other cultures. Italian cookery obtained both its pasta and its rice from China, courtesy of Marco Polo. Spanish cuisine is in large measure Moorish, i.e. Arab-influenced — as, indeed, is the whole Western structure of a meal with a soup to start with, small appetising *hors d'oeuvres*, more substantial main dishes and a sweet dessert at the end, not to mention coffee. All these traditions came to Spain with the Moors in the 8th century, evolved during the heyday of Moorish civilisation and were spread in the course of the Renaissance, with the Spanish court ceremonial, to countries where the Hapsburgs married into royal families — virtually the whole of Europe. Classic British cookery is full of elements from the former colonies, and so forth.

Cross-cooking has consistently been the dominant evolutionary principle of global gastronomy. It was not until French cuisine became pre-eminent, with its increasing stranglehold, in the late 19th century that this evolution came to a standstill — for a century. Escoffier's recipe collection, above all, became an Old Testament of the culinary art that one was sup-posed to follow to the letter. The skill of a *chef de cuisine* in Oslo or New York was appraised on the basis of his ability to replicate the old French recipes, not to make the best of local raw produce. Naturally, the results never matched those in Paris.

This almost totalitarian *ancien régime* began to crumble at the end of the 1970s with the emergence of *nouvelle cuisine*, which represented a rebellion against the old cuisine and, in particular, embraced innovation and local raw materials. With the idea of *cuisine de marché* — creating meals by using the best raw produce available at any time — the decline of the French gastronomic empire began. Culinary artists worldwide began rediscovering fine local raw materials, and exciting and advanced national cooking styles were soon flourishing in Germany, Scandinavia, Britain, the USA and Australia —

formerly devoted dominions of France.

With reinforced self-esteem, more and more people also began to use flavourings and ideas from other parts of the world — especially the Orient.

Chinese and Indian restaurants had, of course, long existed in large parts of the West, often in fairly insipid and modified forms. But in the 1980s came the great breakthrough for 'exotic' cuisines. Now, vapid flavours were no longer sought after. The Japanese led the way; sushi, with its pungent *wasabi*, still holds sway. Next came chili-hot 'Tex-Mex' cookery, sweeping across the world like a prairie fire and leaving behind, like its successor the 'cajun' wave, an abundance of soot and scorched palates. Then came the Thai trend, which still prevails — even in Asia, where the major cities are highly susceptible to fashion. Thai cooking opened the door for other Asian cuisines: Vietnamese, Indonesian, Korean and Malaysian.

Some of these oriental cuisines had themselves always been eclectic. Malaysian cookery, for example, includes Chinese, Thai, Indian, Indonesian and Arab (Malaysia is officially a Muslim country) elements. Vietnamese cooking — now enjoying worldwide triumphs — is also composite in origin, with its legacies from many foreign rulers, especially the French and Chinese.

PACIFIC COOKERY, ANOTHER ECLECTIC CUISINE that has evolved on both sides of the ocean more or less simultaneously, today inspires the whole world.

From being the world's last outpost — in culinary terms, a real backwater — Australia has now emerged as one of the world's foremost 'foodie' nations. In South Australia's capital Adelaide, with the great

Niclas Ryhnell is one of the skilful culinary artists at Norrlands Bar & Grill.

Barossa Valley wine district close by, a few restaurants began to apply Asian techniques to fine local produce in the mid-1970s. Soon a new, eclectic cuisine was flourishing in several Australian cities. But Adelaide can probably claim to be the birthplace of modern Pacific cooking.

Many Californians would protest, and assert that the birth took place in Los Angeles. The Austrian Wolfgang Puck is, admittedly, the legend of modern Pacific cuisine. In the 1970s, he was already the eminent chef of Ma Maison in Los Angeles. But it was not until the formidable success of Spago (1982) and Chinois on Main (1983) that Puck gained full scope for his combinatory skills. Spago, a radically

'One flew East, one flew West, one flew over the cookery nest.' A three-course meal with exotic extravaganzas by Bröderna Dahlbom.

modern and informal restaurant, shocked many by serving both pizza and *foie gras*, and Chinois on Main married two of the world's foremost cuisines – the Chinese and the French. The term 'cross-cooking' was coined.

California, with its natural perspective on West and East alike and its unprejudiced consumers, rapidly became the most vibrant venue for cross-cooking. Here, in rapid succession, eating-places opened under such designations as 'Franco-Japonais', 'Chino-Latino', 'Mexi-Italiano' and other combinations of all kinds, conceivable and otherwise. East may be East and West West, but here the twain certainly meet on the restaurant plate.

Today, Pacific cookery too has matured. Its culinary techniques are largely Italian: risotto, pasta, carpaccio and the like are conspicuous starting points. Vegetables no longer feature in walk-on parts, but in leading roles and sometimes solo acts. Highly colourful fruit is used in salads and sauces alike, imparting strong natural sweetness and acidity to many dishes. Fish and poultry have pride of place, with quadripeds coming a poor second. Japanese elements like *tempura* and *sashimi* are present, as are oriental spices and Mexican chilis in varying strengths. Everything is prepared with a light touch – there is no protracted stewing; most dishes seem but briefly acquainted with the pan, grill or oven – and the visual impact is striking.

EUROPE, TOO, CAN CLAIM PIONEERING CONTRIbutions to contemporary cross-cooking. One of the true pioneers was the restaurant Mr Chow in London. By the late 1970s, superb cooking was already under way here on the nouvelle chinoise theme. Here, classic Chinese recipes were reinterpreted, sometimes with a blend of typical European raw materials and, above all, in a highly aesthetic and innovative dramaturgic presentation.

French culinary artists have continued throughout to build on their own traditions and, accordingly, kept away from the global eclectic trend to a high degree. However, they have cast the odd acquisitive glance at Chinese cookery, in particular, which has always been prized by the French: classics like *canard lacqué*, after all, have Chinese prototypes.

Otherwise, it is primarily the Mediterranean – from Catalonia to Italy, Turkey, Lebanon and North Africa – that inspires cooks in Europe nowadays: rustic local traditions rather than urban elegance, and Provence rather than Paris. Mediterranean cuisine is attractive, tasty, healthful and neither unduly costly nor complicated. In other words it has been well suited to the informal and oft impecunious 1990s.

In Scandinavia it is, above all, Italian culinary arts that have dominated trends. This is by no means unique: Italian cuisine has enjoyed tremendous popularity worldwide throughout the decade, and is actually on the way to ousting its French counterpart as the dominant model. Typically enough, it is now Italian – not French – restaurants that are the most fashionable and expensive at the new luxury hotels all over the world, especially in East Asia.

We are, perhaps, even heading for a new international cuisine in which restaurants worldwide, with equal predictability, serve carpaccio with olive oil and sliced Parmesan, *osso bucco* and *tiramisu*, just as they once served lobster bisque, Sole Walewska and Crêpes Suzette.

What's Cooking in the Air?

THE WINE IS COOLING, THE TABLES ARE laid. There are fresh cut flowers in the vases, the food is on the cooker and the uniformed staff are ready to take the guests' orders. Just like at any other good restaurant. The only difference is that this restaurant has hundreds of different dining rooms – which, instead of being stationary, take off and head for the most far-flung parts of the world several times a day.

Welcome to the SAS Flight Kitchen, which serves nearly 20 million guests a year. The kitchen work-force, too, is unusually large: Gate Gourmet, which supplies the food for SAS in Scandinavia, has 800 employees in Stockholm, 500 in Oslo and 1,000 in Copenhagen. SAS also has other high-class food suppliers at some 100 locations around the world.

It was another matter in SAS's carefree youth, at the end of the 1940s. In those days, the air hostesses or pursers themselves went out and bought the raw materials before the aircraft took off. Meals were prepared in a small pantry in the cabin, and served sumptuously according to the example of the airline's major competitor at the time, the luxury liner Queen Elizabeth. On SAS's first service to New York, among the meals provided were, for example, a self-service *smörgåsbord*, Angels on horseback (mussels wrapped in bacon), *Poularde rôtie* (roast spring chicken) with French fries, a mixed salad and ice-cream parfait.

After a few years SAS was the first airline to introduce two classes on its intercontinental flights. The minimum requirement in first class was caviare, *foie gras* and champagne. In tourist class, passengers usually had to content themselves with tinned ham.

The tone dictated by the Queen Elizabeth is still echoed in most international flight kitchens. The fact is that the airline industry has become one of the last bastions of 'international cuisine', the anonymous global cooking style rooted in classic French cookery that dominated the international restaurant scene for almost a century. On the ground, however, it died out early in the 1980s when *nouvelle cuisine* placed local raw materials in focus, and the modern phenomenon of 'cross-cooking' (see page 10) was the nail in its coffin.

Gate Gourmet employs a staff of 2,300 in Scandinavia.

Over the years, SAS has been responsible for many innovations in the air, especially with regard to food. The *smørrebrød* war is famous. In 1954 SAS began serving generous Danish *smørrebrød* buffets in tourist class on North Atlantic flights. According to IATA's regulations the airlines were not allowed to serve free meals, but only simple English-style sandwiches. SAS's 'open sandwiches' were heaped with pâté, salmon, roast beef and other 'cooked' delicacies, just as they were served in Denmark. American airlines protested vociferously and demanded that SAS forfeit its flying rights unless it stopped serving the free *smørrebrød*. In due course SAS was fined, but also given permission to go on serving these delicacies as long as a square inch of the bread showed at one corner. Today, open sandwiches are served by many airlines – but only rarely by SAS, which has moved on.

With Scandinavian World Cooking, SAS is again innovating in the flight kitchen. Without abandoning the Scandinavian foundation we can, in this eclectic cuisine, make use of exciting techniques and local raw materials in various countries – a kind of global *cuisine de marché*. What, in fact, could be more suitable than a composite basis when one has both guests and suppliers from all over the world?

If a particular vegetable is prevalent in Italy in September, it may well turn up on the plates on outgoing flights from that country. Fresh vegetables have been transformed from decoration and garnishes to basic raw produce. More vegetables, a lighter touch at the cooker and less fat are cornerstones of SAS Scandinavian World Cooking. Fresher, lighter, more wholesome food is what many passengers have long demanded.

Simmering in the pans in Bologne, Delhi, Bangkok, Seattle, Frankfurt, Moscow and some 95 other cities worldwide are various versions of Scandinavian World Cooking. Trying to harmonise these cuisines while leaving scope for local improvisations and raw materials is both a culinary and an organisational challenge – and a constant source of inspiration and further development.

SAS's new food concept is an aerial counterpart of what good contemporary restaurants are serving in Scandinavia and many world metropolises.

Nonetheless, Scandinavian World Cooking turns many of the fundamental rules of airline cooking upside down. If classic in-flight meals have given priority to fairly neutral food 'that as few as possible can dislike', SAS Scandinavian World Cooking entails a higher level of risk – more advanced food with a taste 'that as many as possible can like', well aware that some people may, perhaps, not like it at all.

VERY EARLY IN THE MORNING, BEFORE THE STAFF have arrived and while the bakery is still deserted, the refrigerator is automatically transformed into a proofing chamber. The dough baked during the evening shift starts rising, in order for travellers on the morning flight to be served freshly baked bread for breakfast.

A new day has started at Gate Gourmet, the company in charge of the baking, cold cuts and cooking at Arlanda, near Stockholm.

The setting could be taken from the TV series Star Trek: people in white uniforms move through doors that swish open automatically, all the heavy jobs are automated, computer consoles seem to be blinking everywhere, and there is a constant ring of mobile telephones. The atmosphere is charged with an incessant flow of information: how many passengers there are on each flight, what position each food cabinet is to occupy on the aircraft, and whether any passenger wishes to have something that is not on the regular menu.

For the logistics, too, a global approach is necessary. An international airline like SAS flies on its own wings to more than 100 destinations. And SAS's passengers do not want to feel there is no escape from the same chicken kebab all round the world. The menus are therefore rotated according to an ingenious system. Whether you take domestic flights, commute within Scandinavia, change plans or travel on the international routes, you are never served the same dish twice running.

At Gate Gourmet, everything is either very small – beverage cans, chocolate-biscuit packages, peanut bags – or gigantic. The bulky pans on the cooker look as if they belong in giant country, and the ladles are as large as oars. The ovens are reminiscent of old-fashioned wardrobes, and in the enormous sink, bigger than a carwash, both the beer glasses of tourist-class passengers and the EuroClass passengers' Japanese teacups from Tokyo disappear.

But despite the advanced technology the cooking is still a handicraft. In the kitchen, people and smells from all over the world are blended – 'cross-cooking', in a very literal sense, is under way.

When it is time to 'serve' the food, the flight kitchen's 'head waiters' sit at large monitors and direct their 'waitresses' – huge high-loaders, a type of truck in which the whole platform is raised up to the aircraft to deliver food or remove dishes and cutlery for washing.

At the loading ramp for the high-loaders, the food cabinets for flight SK985 to Tokyo are ready for loading. The passengers can choose between American steak and black beans with cajun spices or rice rolls and teriyaki – well separated, since the Japanese never mix the sacred rice with meat or fish. The third option is cod with horseradish butter, Savoy cabbage and potatoes.

A late arrival, a special meal from Hermolis the kosher supplier, is also ready. The meal has been blessed by a rabbi and then sealed. On this particular aircraft, 20 different portions of special food, ordered for religious or health reasons, and four different vegetarian variants, are to be served.

Now it is only the guests who are lacking. But there is no doubt that all the places will be taken this evening. In fact, most tables were booked several weeks in advance...

Journey through Seven Cuisines

WHAT IS 'TYPICAL SCANDINAVIAN FOOD'? The person who, if anyone, knows by now is Severin Sjöstedt, the culinary artist who, with SAS's team of meal planners, co-ordinated and processed all the ideas and visions that emerged during the work on Scandinavian World Cooking, SAS's new meal concept.

'Yes, indeed, there is a strong Scandinavian culinary tradition and it contains marked national features,' says Sjöstedt. 'But today we all live in a multi-cultural milieu, and this spells rich cross-fertilisation, especially in cookery. We apply new knowledge to processing of our classic raw materials, and we've mastered many ingredients and flavourings from other cultures. But this knowledge of other culinary traditions has also made us understand and appreciate what is distinctive and unique in our own. We're not changing the fundamentals of Scandinavian cuisine: on the contrary, we're taking it out into the world.'

With chefs Niklas Ryhnell and Johan Ahlstedt, Severin Sjöstedt runs one of Stockholm's most celebrated restaurants, the Norrlands Bar & Grill, which has a style of cooking very close to the new food concept adopted by SAS. At Norrlands, Swedish and Mediterranean traditions above all mingle on the plates, but are joined by more far-flung gastronomic elements as well. Here, too, old classics – such as the saffron pancake of Gotland, presented in modern fashion like a muffin – are recreated.

The chefs at Norrlands are fond of 'crossing' fish and meat in modern 'surf & turf' versions. Oven-baked North Sea cod with sauerkraut, grilled pork, red-wine sauce and beef marrow are in many ways typical of the establishment.

'You could more or less call it a Norwegian-Danish-French combination,' says Sjöstedt.

Anders Lauring in Oslo is, at all events, Scandinavia personified:

Severin Sjöstedt.

Anders Lauring.

Eyvind Hellstrøm.

born in Denmark and married to a Swede, he now lives in Norway, where he has been running the restaurant Kastanjen in Oslo for several years. His motley background is clearly apparent in his language — he actually speaks 'cross-Scandinavian', an unusual blend of all three languages.

If Lauring himself is a hybrid, the pots and pans that simmer in his kitchen are so to an even higher degree. Eating at Kastanjen is a voluptuous adventure. The combinations are frequently bold and the flavours stark. What about, for example, grilled tuna with *wasabi* potato purée, soy sauce and ginger, or a version of the Peruvian *ceviche* made of salmon and cod, served with Indian papadams?

'I'm inspired by Mediterranean cookery and the modern dining-out scene in London, for example. But you have to base it on local produce, and work with existing conditions.'

'Nor must it be too expensive. I'm scared stiff that the restaurant will be perceived as too refined and exclusive. It would be so dull here then,' he says, casting a glance over the far from formal dining room, with its warm and welcoming atmosphere and numerous artistic wrought-iron embellishments.

In the Kastanjen kitchen, the atmosphere is exuberant and democratic. Although Anders Lauring is the boss, all the five chefs employed on a normal evening join in the creative process. Incessantly, they stir one another's pans, engage in discussion and exchange mutual criticism and praise while the evening's dishes are being prepared.

An entirely different discipline prevails at Eyvind Hellstrøm's restaurant Bagatelle, a little further down the same Oslo street. The maestro himself orchestrates raw materials and staff alike with a sure hand. Everything and everyone — from the specially imported *foie gras* to the French dessert virtuoso — know their allotted parts. This is a prerequisite for the precision cooking, at the height of gastronomic proficiency, that is pursued here.

Bagatelle is, accordingly, the only restaurant in Scandinavia to date that has succeeded in earning two stars in the Guide Michelin — and the only one in the world that has managed to achieve this distinction without silver cutlery in its table settings. One of the stars has now fallen by the wayside, perhaps after the French tyre manufacturer's inspectors

Bo Jacobsen.

CHAPTER IV

Thomas Drejing.

gave some thought to the question of cutlery.

Eyvind Hellstrøm cannot be bothered with the wildest cross-cooking experiments. But he certainly lets himself be inspired by exotic cuisines, despite his firm opinion that 'French cookery is the universal source'. Such dishes on the Bagatelle menu as asparagus and green summer peas in truffle butter, and wild duck with grilled *foie gras* and fricassee of forest fungi, are typical of this establishment's philosophy.

'The cook's role is, first and foremost, to understand the raw produce. You have to concentrate on what you're doing and, with the right techniques, work your way towards the optimal flavour. The finish is tremendously important: not only should a sauce be an extraordinary taste experience, but it must also be presented in the right way. The overall impression is important.'

This is confirmed when one is sitting in the magnificently flower-embellished dining room at Baga-

telle, where Eyvind's wife Hege Marie is the charming hostess. A look at the wine list reveals that painstaking care extends to the cellar as well: some 30,000 bottles are stored there in the vaults, with temperature and humidity regulated, and many of these are 'worth a detour' in their own right.

A good bit further south in Scandinavia, on the outskirts of Copenhagen, Eyvind Hellstrøm's Danish counterpart, Erwin Lauterbach, runs the Saison Restaurant. These two gentlemen have a great deal in common, especially their appearance – the same majestic Viking stance, slightly sparse beard and glittering blue eyes that can suddenly harden to steel if a younger cook is careless with the knife. They also share a passion for truly fine raw materials, are both fastidious to a fault in their work, and are united in their quest for the ultimate taste experience. Sure enough, they also worked together – in Sweden – many years ago.

But there are also considerable differences. If Hellstrøm stands with at least one foot still on traditional French soil, with a penchant for exclusive delicacies like *foie gras*, truffles and Oscietre caviar, vegetables are the cornerstone of Erwin Lauterbach's cooking.

'Most fish, for example, taste roughly the same, while vegetables vary so much more in character,' he says, tenderly taking his pick of the Hamburg parsley.

He can hold forth *ad infinitum* on how to bring out the sublime flavour of a carrot, or how a piece of fried celery can consign all else to oblivion.

'In the general, slightly chaotic atmosphere of *fin de siècle* that prevails now, with information stress

Erwin Lauterbach.

Jonas & Anders Dahlbom.

wrapped in filo are typical of this restaurant.

Erwin Lauterbach is also something of a gastronomic grand old man and superguru of all Scandinavia. His kitchen is a kind of university, which countless cooks have attended as apprentices before opening their own, acclaimed establishments.

One of these is Bo Jacobsen, who runs Restaurationen in the centre of Copenhagen. He is a chef of a younger vintage — with the same Viking appearance and the same beard, but combined here with long hair in a ponytail. The fact is that Bo Jacobsen looks almost rough-hewn — a 'Kitchen's Angel' — especially in contrast to the interior decoration of Restaurationen, which is startlingly ornate, with an almost feminine fragility.

However, the food is more like Jacobsen himself: generous in quantity, richly flavoured and featuring Danish *hygge* (well-being). Here there is no stinting with the portions, even though the raw materials are exclusive. Counting calories is hardly up Jacobsen's street.

Like his countryman and former mentor, he adapts his work entirely to the season's best produce. Asparagus, for example, is suitable only during the six-week period when it is at its best.

'We should eat food that is right for the country we live in. I get a lot of my inspiration from abroad — from Italy, above all — but not the actual raw materials. At the same time, I think it's a shame that the old traditional homely fare is beginning to disappear.'

This is a man that prepares oxtail with the same natural elegance as he executes guinea-hen with *foie gras* sauce.

and visual effects on the plate as well, I'm trying instead to slow down the tempo and create harmony.'

One should not conclude that Lauterbach is a vegetarian — both meat and fish feature in Saison's menu, but they seldom play the leading roles in his compositions. Globe artichokes in dill umbels, served with steamed fillet of redfish, and sesame-glazed guinea fowl in cabbage leaves with scorzonera

Thomas Drejing, who runs Petri Pumpa on the other side of the Sound – in Lund, in the Swedish province of Skåne, to be more specific – is another of Erwin Lauterbach's former pupils. Today he belongs to the Swedish *crème de la crème*, with several prizes and distinctions to his credit. His culinary art is entirely based on regional products.

The fish comes from the sea, some tens of kilometres away, and the vegetables from organic farmers in the vicinity. Few can bring out the innermost essence of a raw material as well as Drejing. He also has a talent for coaxing superb flavour experiences out of seemingly simple produce like cabbage and root vegetables. Meat is purchased in the form of whole carcases that are then cut and hung by the restaurant itself – because 'it's fun to preserve that kind of handicraft under your own restaurant roof'.

'I'm opposed to canned food,' he says, referring to imported delicacies from France, for example. 'Both *foie gras* and truffles may be delicious, but this area has a tremendously exciting range of produce. It's the combination that is most fun – it's never quite successful decorating with nothing but trendy Italian furniture, even if the pieces may be a pleasure to look at on their own.'

His plate presentations also possess a singular, epic beauty: every item is displayed clearly and conspicuously against a pure, slightly austere background. In such dishes as ragout of lobster, root vegetables and ginger or baked char with coriander apple and vinegar raisins, there is a streak of intellectual *gravitas* – perhaps even gloom à la Ingmar Bergman – rather than the exuberant sensualism of Federico Fellini. It is not for nothing that Petri Pumpa is called 'Scandinavia's most intelligent restaurant'.

The brothers Anders and Jonas Dahlbom in Gothenburg, Sweden's west-coast metropolis, may be seen as a contrast in certain respects. Here, the tone is easygoing and lighthearted. The restaurant itself – dubbed Bröderna Dahlbom ('Dahlbom Bros.'), of course – is decorated in a mirthful mood, but nowhere near comparable to the wealth of imagination and almost ardent aesthetic that characterises the food borne forth from the open kitchen.

The two brothers, who have long accompanied each other throughout their careers and brought home the same prizes in turn, are in synchrony behind the pots and pans, to say the least. It is almost as if the same chef had four arms – a dream, in other words, when the pressure from the dining room hits the roof on a Saturday night. One can also tell that they have fun together by the menu's 'fillet of veal with chili and pineapple glaze', or 'oyster fungi and lime couscous served with baked potato and red-onion kebab' – or why not 'duck-liver terrine with lentil and mango caviar served with sour nut oil'? No gloom here!

The plate presentations are largely vertical in construction, according to the fashion of the day, and one can understand that the brothers did not find it particularly easy revising their recipes along the lines of Scandinavian World Cooking:

'You invariably try to do something creative, inspired and fun, but it wasn't always that easy to achieve with the small cocottes used in the flight kitchen,' they say.

But we think they – like all the other chefs – have succeeded beyond our every expectation.

Jellied lobster with vegetables and marinated potato

LOBSTER
2 lobsters (approx. 1 kg)

STOCK
olive oil
1/4 carrot
1/8 celeriac
1/4 leek
1/2 onion
1 garlic clove
1 sprig of thyme
1/2 red chili
5 black peppercorns
3 tbs tomato purée
2 dl white wine
1/4 dl brandy (to flame)
olive oil

JELLY
1 carrot
1/8 celeriac
1 root of Hamburg (turnip-rooted) parsley
3 sheets gelatine (or 1 1/2 tsp gelatine powder)
lobster meat (from claws and tails)

POTATO
4 small boiled potatoes
1/4 dl balsam vinegar
1/2 tbs chopped parsley
1/4 dl lobster stock
1 bunch of broad-leaved parsley

In the olden days lobster with potatoes was everyday fare for Scandinavian fisherfolk. Here is a refined variation on this theme: lobster boiled in a rich stock, covered in clear jelly, with marinated potato.

* Kill the lobsters by stabbing them in the head with a knife. Remove the stomach. Break off the claws and divide the lobsters into halves. Refrigerate the claws and tails.
* Chop up the head, shell and carcase and brown in olive oil with finely chopped vegetables and herbs.
* When everything is heated through, add the tomato purée. Stir, pour on the brandy, flame and add the white wine.
* Pour on water to cover, and salt lightly.
* Bring to the boil, skim thoroughly and continue boiling for another approx. 15 minutes.
* Leave the stock to stand for an hour. Then strain it through a fine cloth.

* Boil up the stock again and simmer the claws and tails for about 8 minutes.
* Lift the lobster out of the stock, break the claw shells and carefully remove the meat. Pick out the tail meat, and cut the lobster meat into attractive hunks. Save the claws for garnishing.

* Cook the cleaned, evenly diced vegetables in the lobster stock. Remove them and strain the stock again.
* Reduce the stock to approx. 4 decilitres. Season to taste with salt and pepper if necessary. Put aside 1/4 decilitre of the stock for the potatoes.

* Soak the sheets of gelatine (if used) in cold water for 10 minutes, and then squeeze out the water. Melt the gelatine in the hot stock. Strain the stock once more through a fine cloth.
* Put the lobster and vegetables in cocotte moulds and pour on enough lobster stock to cover. Put in the refrigerator for 3–4 hours to set.

* Mix the balsam vinegar, the saved lobster stock and chopped parsley. Slice the potatoes and pour the marinade on top.

* Serve the turned-out jellies surrounded by lobster meat and marinated potato. Garnish with broad-leaved parsley.

Crayfish-marinated salmon with potato salad

An agreeable cold dish, perfect for serving on sunny summer days. The flowering heads or umbels of dill provide the essential seasoning in the cooking of crayfish. Here it is used in a marinade, in which the salmon is left for 24 hours before being gently poached or steamed. Thus no crayfish are needed for this recipe: it is the dill and salt that give the salmon its 'crayfish flavour'.

* Mix the sugar, salt and water in a saucepan, add half the dill and boil for approx. 20 minutes. Set aside to cool.
* Strain the liquid, snip in the rest of the dill and add the salmon pieces. Refrigerate for approx. 24 hours.
* Put the salmon in a sauté pan, pour on enough liquid to cover the bottom and steam the salmon gently without a lid for approx. 5 minutes, depending on the thickness of the pieces. The salmon should be raw in the middle, and the flesh should be 'flaky' and succulent.
* Lift out the salmon and chill until it is served.

* Boil, peel and slice the potatoes. Lay them in a bowl.
* Rinse the radishes, and slice them thinly.
* Mix the olive oil and vinegar, and season with salt and coarsely ground pepper from the mill.
* Pour the marinade over the potatoes while they are still hot, and mix in the radishes and chives.
* Stand the potatoes in a cool place for approx. 1 hour before serving.

* Flavour the crème fraîche with lemon, finely chopped dill, salt and freshly ground white pepper.
* Divide the potato salad between four plates, add the salmon and garnish with the frilly-leaved endive and sprigs of dill. Dollop a little crème fraîche around the salmon.

SALMON
600 g farmed salmon, in pieces
5 dl water
2 tbs sea salt
1 tbs sugar
30 g fresh dill (preferably umbels)

POTATO SALAD
8 potatoes
1 bunch of radishes
3 tbs olive oil
1 tbs red-wine vinegar
salt and coarsely ground pepper
1 bunch of chives, finely chopped

DRESSING
2 dl crème fraîche
1 tbs lemon juice
1 tbs finely chopped dill
salt and white pepper

ACCOMPANIMENTS
1 head of frilly-leaved endive
sprigs of dill

Parma ham and
mozzarella sandwiches

Italian cuisine has been well established in Scandinavia for so long as to be hardly considered 'foreign' any more. These 'Italian' sandwiches, in all their simplicity, make a superb snack or hors d'œuvre.

∗ Mix the ingredients for the dressing in a blender.
∗ Butter the slices of bread.
∗ Place alternating layers of ham, mozzarella, onion and tomato on half the slices, pour the dressing on top and cap with the remaining slices. Cut each sandwich diagonally and serve as filled triangles.

SANDWICHES
8 slices white bread
butter for spreading
100–200 g Parma ham,
   thinly sliced
400 g mozzarella
3–4 tomatoes, sliced
1 red onion, sliced

DRESSING
2 dl olive oil
1 tbs Dijon mustard
1 tbs vinegar
fresh basil
salt, pepper and sugar to
   taste

With its many interesting restaurants, Gothenburg challenges Stockholm's claim to be Sweden's gastronomic capital.

Clear tomato bouillon
with grilled scallops

This clear tomato soup, with the highly refined garnish of freshly grilled scallops, is rich in flavour if not in hue. Here, the Norwegian variety of scallops, *haneskjell* — relatively small, but all the more delicious for that — are used.

* Slice the tomatoes.
* Mix the sugar and salt, and season the tomatoes before placing them in a fine sieve over a bowl. Leave to drain overnight.

* Brush the scallops with oil and season with salt, pepper and coriander. Grill on one side only, to allow each scallop to keep a firm, raw core. Drain off the oil on a cloth or kitchen paper.

* Heat up the tomato bouillon and dish up in warmed bowls.
* In each bowl, place a small pile of tomato, celery and basil in the middle and arrange the grilled scallops around it.

Contemporary European. It could be anywhere, but it happens to be Oslo.

BOUILLON
1 1/2 kg ripe tomatoes
1 tbs salt
1 tbs sugar

ACCOMPANIMENTS
20 scallops
oil
salt, pepper and coriander
  to taste
basil, finely chopped
tomatoes, peeled and finely
  chopped
celery, finely shredded

Saddle of rabbit with herb stuffing, saffron stock and grilled vegetables

The sweetish rabbit meat takes on a distinctive character from the aniseed-flavoured fennel and the mildly yellow saffron stock. If you feel unsure about how to debone a saddle of rabbit, the butcher or other supplier can no doubt help you.

* Debone the saddle, as far as the ribs, and remove the inner fillet.

* Chop the rabbit carcase and cut the carrot, onion, garlic and leek into pieces. Put them in a pan with the bay leaves and thyme and add enough water to cover.
* Simmer for 3 hours, skimming from time to time.
* Strain the stock and continue boiling until reduced to approx. 4 decilitres.
* Flavour with saffron, coarsely chopped coriander, salt and pepper. Keep hot until serving.

* Spread out the outer fillet and cover with a layer of coarsely chopped parsley. Then place the inner fillet in the middle and roll up the meat in an oblong roll. Tie up with string.
* Rub in salt and freshly ground white pepper, and fry the roll in a little butter until golden brown in a frying pan.

* Finish off in a slow oven, at 130°C, for approx. 5 minutes. Take out the roll, wrap it in foil and keep it hot.

* Clean the fennel, peel the shallots and blanch them in boiling, lightly salted water. Chill them, dry them with a cloth and then brush the fennel and shallots with the olive oil.
* Peel the sweet peppers using a potato peeler, cut them up and scorch a decorative grid pattern onto them in a hot steak grill.

* Cut the rabbit roll into centimetre-thick slices and arrange them in soup dishes with the vegetables. Pour the hot stock on top and garnish with a little coriander. Sprinkle with a modicum of olive oil, if desired, and serve.

RABBIT
1 whole rabbit, skinned and prepared
1 small bunch of parsley
salt and white pepper to taste

STOCK
carcase of rabbit (see above)
1 carrot
1 onion
1 leek
1/2 garlic bulb
bay leaves
thyme
1 sprig of fresh coriander
1/2 g saffron
salt and white pepper to taste

VEGETABLES
1 yellow sweet pepper
1 red sweet pepper
2 small fennel bulbs
12 small shallots
olive oil for frying

Salmon carpaccio with cos lettuce and Västerbotten cheese

A classic Italian dish, made of Scandinavian raw ingredients. *Väster-botten*, here used instead of Parmesan, is a matured and tasty Swedish cheese of very high quality. The fish can be sliced in its frozen state (for the thinnest possible slices) and flavoured with a dressing of olive oil, lime and basil.

* Freeze the salmon and then cut it into extremely thin slices (or ask your fishmonger to help).

* Rinse the lettuce and endive well and leave to dry on kitchen paper.
* Mix the dressing and season to taste.
* Arrange the lettuce and endive leaves on four plates, spread out the salmon and brush with the dressing.

* Lay sliced *Västerbotten* on top and garnish with thin slices of lime and basil leaves.

Gate Gourmet has contributed several recipes of its own, and puts all the other culinary creators' ideas into daily practice.

FISH
400 g lightly salted salmon
100 g Västerbotten cheese
1/2 lime, thinly sliced

LETTUCE
cos (romaine) lettuce
frilly-leaved endive
4 sprigs of basil

DRESSING
1 1/2 dl olive oil
juice of 1/2 lime
1 tsp basil paste (available
  ready-made)
salt and pepper

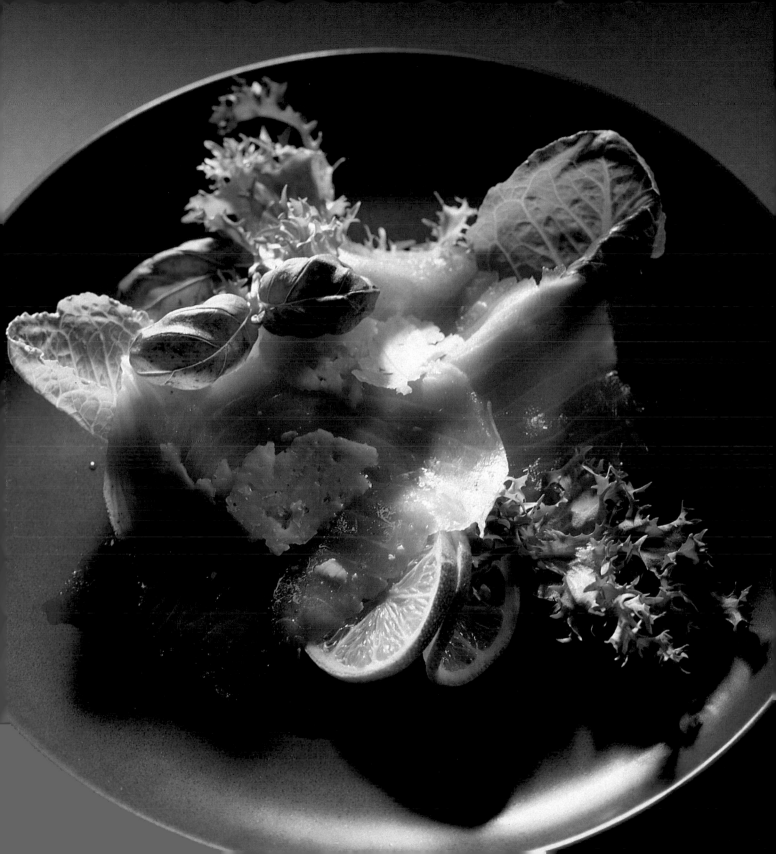

Scallops au gratin
with marinated lemon segments

Haneskjell is the Norwegian name of the scallops fished around the Lofoten islands. These mussels are slightly smaller than those found elsewhere. The marinated segments of lemon go well with many fish and shellfish dishes. They should be left for 14 days to assume the right strength and flavour.

∗ Open the scallops and detach the meat from the shells.
∗ Melt the butter and discard the turbid brown dregs.
∗ Put the grated lemon rind in the butter.
∗ Return the scallops to their shells, pour on the lemon butter and place in an oven preheated to 200°C. Leave for 3 minutes so that the shells and scallops become hot.
∗ Coarsely grind pepper on top, garnish with fresh coriander or parsley and serve immediately.

∗ Quarter the lemons, but do not cut right through. Mix the salt and sugar, and put the mixture into the middle of each lemon. Stand the lemons tightly together in a bowl.

∗ After a couple of days, juice has collected around the lemons. Spoon it over them now and again and chill, preferably for two weeks.
∗ Cut pithless segments out of the lemons and fry them in butter, until attractively golden brown, just before serving.

His Master's Touch: Eyvind Hellstrøm and Terje Ness at Bagatelle.

SCALLOPS
24 fresh scallops
100 g melted, clarified butter
grated rind of 1 lemon
black pepper, coarsely ground
fresh coriander or parsley

LEMON WEDGES
1 kg lemons
30 g sugar
30 g salt
butter for frying

MENU
No. 1

By BO JACOBSEN
Restaurationen

Sugar-salted saffron cod
with marinated chicory sala

Poulard breasts with
morel sauce and fried
rosemary polenta

Mocha cake
with coffee sauce

RECIPES ON PAGES 42–44

Sugar-salted saffron cod
with marinated chicory salad

The practice of 'sugar-salting' raw fish, with various other seasonings, is an old Scandinavian tradition. The best-known dish is, of course, *gravlax* — raw sugar-salted salmon seasoned with dill — but the method can also be applied to other kinds of fish. Here, raw cod is seasoned with salt, sugar and also a little saffron, which imparts both an attractive colour and extra flavour.

FISH
1 cod fillet with skin,
   approx. 600 g
4 tbs salt
5 tbs sugar
1/2 g saffron

SALAD
3 heads of chicory
juice of 1 lemon
1 tbs salt
1/4 tsp white pepper
1/3 dl olive oil
finely chopped parsley

SAFFRON CREAM
1 dl crème fraîche
1 tsp French mustard
1/4 dl white wine
1 pinch of crushed saffron
salt and pepper to taste

* Fillet the cod and pick out all the bones, but leave the skin on.
* Lay the fish in an oblong dish, meat side up.
* Mix the salt, sugar and saffron, and sprinkle it over the fish. Cover with foil and refrigerate for 24 hours.

* Finely shred the chicory and mix with lemon juice, salt and pepper. Put a light weight on the salad and refrigerate for 24 hours or so.

* Pour away the liquid that has collected, and stir in olive oil just before serving.

* Cut the cod into thin diagonal slices free from skin.
* Dish up the slices so that the saffron-yellow outer edges form a pattern around the salad, which is placed in the middle of each plate. Sprinkle with a little parsley to garnish.

* Mix the saffron cream, pour it into a bowl and serve as a side dish.

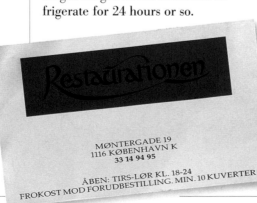

Restaurationen

MØNTERGADE 19
1116 KØBENHAVN K
33 14 94 95

ÅBEN: TIRS-LØR KL. 18-24
FROKOST MOD FORUDBESTILLING. MIN. 10 KUVERTER

Poulard breasts with morel sauce and fried rosemary polenta

In Denmark large, fat young hens — poulards — are raised for their tender, succulent meat. This recipe uses only the breasts, which are ample for four people. The accompanying morels are a seductive but insidious delicacy: every species in the genus is poisonous, but correct handling reduces the danger — and they taste superb.

* Soak the morels in water for an hour or more. Discard the water.
* Peel and finely chop the shallots, and fry gently in butter without browning. Add the mushroom stock and boil until reduced to 1/2 decilitre.
* Season to taste with salt, pepper and Madeira. Stir in a dab of butter and add the morels, cut into slices.

* Bring to the boil 5 decilitres of water and stir in the cornmeal, a little at a time. Simmer over gentle heat for approx. 20 minutes, stirring frequently. If the polenta becomes too thick, dilute with a little water.
* When the polenta is ready, with a consistency resembling rice pudding, add the Parmesan, chopped rosemary and olive oil. Season with salt and pepper and stir in the butter.
* Spread out the polenta in a straight-sided dish, in a layer approx. 1 1/2 cm thick. Cover with plastic foil and set the polenta aside to cool.

* Simmer the poulard breasts gently in stock until they are fully cooked. Then slice them and divide between four plates. Keep them hot.

* Cut out pieces of polenta (allowing three per person) and fry them in butter until they are an attractive golden brown. Dish up, and pour on the morel sauce. If whole morels are available, they make a splendid — and tasty — decoration.

POULTRY
2 poulard breasts
  (approx. 600 g)
stock
  (perhaps from the carcase)
salt and white pepper

MOREL SAUCE
10 g dried morels
2 dl mushroom stock
  (available in cubes)
1 shallot
20 g butter + butter for frying
salt and pepper
1/2 dl Madeira

POLENTA
30 g coarsely ground
  cornmeal (polenta)
5 dl water
20 g grated Parmesan
1 sprig of rosemary
1/4 dl olive oil
salt and pepper to taste
20 g butter + butter for frying

Mocha cake
with coffee sauce

A truly delicious dessert with almonds, chocolate and a coffee flavour from whole coffee beans. The mixture for the cake consists of ready-made almond paste covered with flaked almonds: a perfect way to round off the meal.

CAKE
45 g almond paste
3 tbs milk
1/2 egg white
3 tbs sugar
10 g flaked almonds

MOCHA CREAM
2 dl whipping cream
100 g white block chocolate
30 g whole coffee beans

COFFEE SAUCE
3/4 dl strong, freshly
   brewed coffee
1 1/2 tbs sugar
1/2 tbs cornflour (maizena)

* Mix the almond paste with the milk until smooth.
* Whisk the egg white with the sugar as for meringue, and fold it into the almond paste.
* Spread the paste out on oven paper on a baking tin, and cover with flaked almonds. Bake in the oven at 175°C until the almonds are an attractive golden brown.

* Bring the cream to the boil, and melt the chocolate in it. Pour the chocolate cream over the whole coffee beans and leave to stand for approx. 6 hours, so that the cream absorbs plenty of flavour from the beans.
* Strain and chill the sauce before whisking it to a creamy consistency.

* For the coffee sauce, bring the strong brewed coffee to the boil, add sugar and thicken with cornflour. Whisk until cooled.

* Cut out even-sized pieces of almond cake and sandwich them together in pairs with the mocha cream. Serve the cake surrounded with coffee sauce.

Big man in small kitchen – Bo Jacobsen at Restaurationen.

Raw beetroot with horseradish salad and sliced apple

It is advisable to prepare a large quantity of marinated beetroot — it keeps well, and makes a suitable accompaniment to many dishes. For long-term storage, adding new seasonings to taste may be necessary. If a completely vegetarian dish is not desired, a slice of smoked Danish herring can with advantage be served alongside.

* Peel and cut the raw beetroot into thin slices, using a mandolin or grater.
* Whisk together the ingredients for the marinade and season it to taste with salt and pepper.
* Pour the marinade over the beetroot and leave to stand for a few hours. To serve, add the finely chopped shallot.

* For the salad, stir the cream and lemon juice gently until the mixture thickens. Adjust the consistency and flavour with more cream or lemon if necessary. Season with salt, pepper and grated horseradish.

* Core the apples and then cut them into very thin segments.
* Fry the apple segments in grape oil until slightly browned, and pour on the vinegar.
* Keep the apples hot until they are served.

* Mix the different varieties of lettuce, well rinsed and dried, with the horseradish dressing. The simplest method is to pour the horseradish dressing into a large bowl and distribute it around and up the sides. Then add the lettuce leaves and toss them in the bowl with the herbs to mix everything thoroughly. Add salt if desired.

* Lay the beetroot in a ring on each plate, leaving room for the salad in the middle.
* To give the salad an airy appearance, press it down with the hot apple slices in a fairly deep circular mould that is then lifted away just before serving.
* Sprinkle with finely chopped shallot.
* Serve with a slice of bread fried in a pan with a little smoked oil, or on toast, with a slice of smoked fish on top.

BEETROOT
200 g beetroot, raw

MARINADE
1 dl grape oil
juice of 1 lemon
2 garlic cloves, pressed
1 shallot, finely chopped
salt and pepper to taste

SALAD
mixed lettuce varieties
1 dl whipping cream
2 tbs lemon juice
grated horseradish
2 apples, thinly sliced
1 tbs white-wine vinegar
salt and pepper to taste
fresh herbs in season

ACCOMPANIMENTS
4 tbs shallot, finely chopped
4 slices fried bread
4 tbs smoked olive oil

Crab soup with saffron and scallop quenelles

Tiny shore crabs have more flavour under their shells than one could possibly believe. In this soup, the marine taste is accentuated with saffron and a hint of cayenne. The delicious quenelles of scallops and scampi are the highlight of this dish.

SOUP
1 kg live shore crabs
olive oil
2 litres water
1 carrot
50 g celeriac
1/2 leek
1 onion
4 garlic cloves
1/2 sachet saffron (1/4 gram)
150 g butter
salt, pepper and cayenne
  to taste

QUENELLES
100 g meat from scallops
100 g meat from scampi
1 dl whipping cream
1 egg
salt and pepper
ginger and cayenne to taste
stock for boiling

ACCOMPANIMENTS
garlic bread fried in butter
shredded basil
boiled whipped cream

* Rinse the live shore crabs in cold water. Drain.
* Heat up oil 1 centimetre deep in a saucepan. Add the crabs. Cover, and shake the pan from time to time. Boil for 10 minutes until all the crabs are red.

* Break the crabs with a wooden club.
* Boil up 2 litres of water and put in the cut-up vegetables with the crab fragments. Boil for approx. 45 minutes, stirring the pan now and then. Set aside to cool.
* Mix everything in the blender. Strain through a fine sieve and transfer to a slightly smaller saucepan. Reduce until 1 litre remains.
* Add saffron and thicken with butter just before serving. Season to taste with salt, pepper and a pinch of cayenne.

* Make sure the blender knives are sharp, since this stage should not take long. When fish and shellfish are puréed all the ingredients should be very cold (the same applies to the actual blender), and preparation should be rapid. Otherwise, the mixture may separate.
* Place equal quantities of meat from scallops and scampi in the blender and add salt, a beaten egg and the cream, pouring it in a thin stream. Run the blender until the mixture is smooth and malleable.
* Season with salt, pepper, a little ginger (fresh or ground) and a pinch of cayenne to taste.
* Shape the mixture into small, oblong quenelles and simmer them gently in stock for approx. 3 minutes.

* Dice white bread. Fry the dice in clarified butter and flavour with garlic. Drain the crisp dice (croutons) on kitchen paper and then serve them with the soup. Garnish with a coil of boiled, whipped cream and basil leaves.

Smoked salmon roulades on dark rye bread

A modern version of a genuine Scandinavian classic. Here, the traditional smoked salmon on *kavring* — a dark, slightly sour type of rye bread — is combined with cream cheese and lime. A simple hors d'œuvre that can be prepared in advance.

* Blanch the scallions in boiling water.
* Mix the oil and vinegar and season with chives, salt and pepper.
* Marinate the onions for a while in the vinaigrette: the longer, the richer the flavour.

* Season the cream cheese with the lime.
* Spread a layer of cheese on each slice of salmon, roll it up and stand it on the buttered bread.
* Garnish with the scallions and serve.

From the dining room, you can watch work in progress in the Bröderna Dahlbom's open kitchen in Gothenburg.

OPEN SANDWICHES
200 g smoked salmon in slices
4 slices of kavring
butter for spreading
200 g plain cream cheese
  (e.g. Philadelphia)
rind and juice of 1 lime
4 small, slender scallions/
  spring onions, sliced
1 tbs olive oil
1 tbs vinegar
chives, finely chopped
salt and pepper to taste

Lobster on boiled lettuce in pasta, with almond flakes and butter pesto

A magnificent lobster can be served either solo or with intricate accompaniments, as in this sophisticated *hors d'œuvre*. The recipe is no child's play but the result, with an impressive array of refinements on each plate, is all the more delectable for that.

* Boil the lobsters one at a time in salted water for approx. 2 minutes.
* Then cool them in cold water.
* Shell and set aside the meat, including that from the claws.

* Hack up the shells and discarded lobster parts and brown them in butter with the diced carrot, onion, leek, celeriac and parsley stalks.
* Boil for about 30 minutes in enough water to cover, strain, and reduce the liquid by half. Add 1 tablespoonful of mild olive oil and the lemon juice.

* Bring plenty of water to the boil in a large saucepan. Add salt and the coarsely cut-up lettuce. Simmer for 5 minutes. Remove the lettuce and drain.
* Heat the butter in a large pan and sauté the lettuce until dry with the chives and tarragon. Season to taste.
* Roll the lettuce in freshly cooked, broad pasta strips (here, one portion suffices for four) just before serving.

* For the pesto, blanch the garlic cloves in boiling water four times, to give the garlic a muted, full taste. Chill.
* Place the basil leaves in a blender with the garlic cloves. Add the (cold, diced) butter gradually, and then the (powdered or finely ground) almonds.
* Just before serving, heat the pesto in a little water. Strain to make it smooth before pouring it over the lobster.

* Mix the flaked almonds with whisked egg white, spread out on oven paper, and bake at 180°C for about 10 minutes until golden brown.
* Detach the lobster meat from the shells, then replace it and heat the filled shells in steam. Dish up on warmed plates with the lettuce pasta and garnish with the almond flakes. Spoon the pesto on top, and drip the lobster gravy around it.

LOBSTER
4 small lobsters
water + salt for boiling

LETTUCE
1 lettuce
salt + water for boiling
butter for browning
2 tbs finely chopped chives
1 tbs finely shredded tarragon
salt and pepper
pasta, preferably fresh

BUTTER PESTO
1 large garlic
1 pot fresh basil
100 g butter
5 g almond powder
   (or corresponding quantity
   of ground almonds)
water

LOBSTER GRAVY
lobster shells
1 carrot
1 onion
1/2 leek
2 tbs finely chopped celeriac
4 parsley stalks
water for boiling
1 tbs olive oil
1 tsp lemon juice

ALMOND FLAKES
150 g flaked almonds
1/2 egg white

Tomato soup with mint

Succulent, ripe tomatoes — by all means somewhat overripe — are suitable for this soup. The main consideration is richness of flavour. The soup is served cold with very finely diced raw vegetables, such as celeriac, courgettes and red peppers. Cold-smoked salmon gives the soup a more Scandinavian touch.

SOUP
500 g sun-ripened tomatoes
3 sprigs of fresh mint
1 onion
approx. 2 dl celeriac,
  finely diced
2 tbs oil
salt and pepper to taste

ACCOMPANIMENTS
1/2 dl celeriac, diced
1/2 dl courgettes, diced
1/2 dl red sweet peppers,
  diced
200 g cold-smoked salmon,
  sliced
4 sprigs of mint

* Dice the onion and celeriac. Cut up the tomatoes.
* Heat up the oil in a saucepan. Add the onion and celeriac and sauté over gentle heat for a few minutes.
* Put in the tomatoes and simmer gently under a lid for approx. 20 minutes. Make sure that the quantity of liquid remains constant throughout — fill up with water if necessary.

* Mix the soup in a blender.

The quantity should be approx. 8 decilitres.
* Season to taste with salt and pepper. Leave to cool.

* Dice the vegetables to serve, and cut the salmon into leaf-thin slices, allowing three slices per person.
* Dish up the soup in plates or bowls. Lay the salmon slices in the middle, sprinkle the raw, diced vegetables on top and stick in a sprig of mint to garnish.

Many of Scandinavia's most renowned culinary artists have been apprenticed to Erwin Lauterbach (centre).

MENU
No. 2

By FLIGHT KITCHEN

Gate Gourmet

Makisushi and Oshisushi

Pork fillet with basil pasta
and sweet peppers baked in thyme

Selected cheeses

Curd cheesecake with
bilberries

RECIPES ON PAGES 58–60

Makisushi
and Oshisushi

Fish eaten raw should preferably come from cold waters. Thus, Scandinavian fish is highly suitable for sushi. Sushi rice is on sale in Asian shops, as is *nori* (seaweed in thin sheets) for *makisushi*. A *makisu*, (straw mat), and *wasabi*, the green Japanese 'horseradish', are also essential.

RICE
3 1/2 dl Japanese rice
7 dl water

VINEGAR MIXTURE
5 tbs rice vinegar
2 tsp salt
1 tbs mirin wine (available in
  Asian shops)
2 tbs sugar
1 tbs glutamate (Ajinomoto)

MAKISUSHI
2 sheets of nori
150 g fresh salmon
1 cucumber
1 avocado
wasabi
boiled sushi rice (see above)

OSHISUSHI
8 thin slices of smoked eel
8 thin slices of smoked or
  fresh salmon
boiled sushi rice (see above)
wasabi

* Wash the rice well in cold water.
* Put the rice in a saucepan, pour on the water and bring to the boil.
* Reduce the heat as far as possible. When the rice has absorbed all the water, put the pan aside. Keep it warm for approx. 2 hours.
* Turn the rice out into a bowl. Work the vinegar mixture in with a rice ladle. Work the rice for 10 minutes, or until elastic.
* The rice should now be lukewarm (37°c). Retain the heat by using a bain-marie.

* Cut the salmon for the makisushi into shreds as long as the nori.
* Peel the avocado and halved cucumber (scrape out the cucumber seeds) and cut them into sticks as long as the nori.
* Lay the nori on the makisu, shiny side down, placing the makisu so that you roll it away from yourself.
* Moisten your hands and spread an even, barely centimetre-thick layer of rice on the nori. Leave about 2 centimetres to seal the roll with.
* Place the salmon, cucumber and avocado sticks, and wasabi in the middle and roll everything up firmly. Moisten the edge of the nori and seal the roll. Leave to stand for a while.
* Cut the roll into 10–12 pieces.

* With your right hand, work 20 grams of rice for the oshisushi into a ball.
* Dip your index finger in the green wasabi paste and draw a line across the underside of the salmon. Put a slice of salmon (and a slice of eel) in your left hand, place the rice ball on top and turn your hand right over, holding the rice ball firmly with your fingers. If it is difficult to place two kinds of topping on the same rice ball, it is better to make two different kinds of sushi instead.
* Adjust the shape of the sushi to the topping to make it even and oblong.

Pork fillet with basil pasta and sweet peppers baked in thyme

An Italian-inspired, truly festive dish with a delicious fillet of pork and flat noodles in a crème fraîche sauce, flavoured with basil and grated Parmesan. Red sweet peppers and shallots seasoned with garlic, balsam vinegar and thyme provide extra colour and flavour.

* Cook the noodles according to the instructions on the pack. Drain them thoroughly and keep them hot.
* Mix the crème fraîche and grated Parmesan. Dilute with a dash of water and flavour with basil paste, a little salt and freshly ground pepper.
* Turn the crème fraîche sauce into the pasta just before serving.

* Grill the sweet peppers under the oven grill. When the skin is charred, pull it off under cold, running water.
* Cut the sweet peppers into large pieces.
* Sauté the shallots in a frying pan with a little oil.
* Press the garlic and add the peeled sweet peppers and thyme (with stalks removed).
* Add the balsam vinegar and season with salt and pepper.

* Cut the pork fillet into 4 pieces and sauté on both sides in equal quantities of butter and oil. Season with salt and pepper.

* Serve the pork fillet with the sweet peppers and noodles on warmed plates.

MEAT
400 g pork fillet
salt and pepper
butter and oil for frying

PASTA
300 g boiled flat noodles
1 1/2 dl crème fraîche
1 dl grated Parmesan
3 tbs water
basil paste, canned
salt and pepper

SWEET PEPPERS
4 large red sweet peppers, grilled and peeled
2 shallots, finely chopped
2 garlic cloves, pressed
4 sprigs of fresh thyme
olive oil
1 tbs balsam vinegar
salt and pepper

Curd cheesecake with bilberries

The curd cheese used here is excellent in desserts, both of the baked kind and those with a delicious filling. Since its fat content is low, curd cheese can be enjoyed by calorie-counters as well. The cake is enough for some 12–14 portions.

CAKE

3 eggs
1 1/2 dl sugar
2 dl plain wheat flour
1 tsp baking powder
  (or use self-raising flour)

FILLING

1 dl milk
1 egg yolk
2 tbs sugar
1 sheet of gelatine (1/2 tsp
  gelatine powder)
2 dl curd cheese
juice of 1/2 lemon
1 dl whipping cream

GARNISHES

3–4 dl bilberries
  (or 1 pack frozen)
1 dl thick fruit sauce
  (available ready-made in
  some countries) or puréed,
  stewed fruit
2 sheets of gelatine
  (1 tsp gelatine powder)

* Beat the eggs and sugar until porous. Gently stir in the flour mixed with the baking powder (or the self-raising flour).
* Cover a baking tin or oven pan with oven paper. Spread the mixture out on the paper and bake in the oven at 250°C for approx. 5 minutes.
* Turn the cake upside down on sugared oven paper and leave it to cool under the baking tin. Pull off the oven paper on which the cake was baked.

* Whisk together the milk, egg yolk and sugar for the filling. Heat, whisking continuously, until it reaches 70°C, when the mixture thickens.
* Soak all three sheets of gelatine (if used) in cold water for approx. 10 minutes, and then squeeze out the liquid. Melt one of the sheets (1/3 of the powder, if used) in the lukewarm mixture and leave to cool.
* Whip the cream, mix it with the curd cheese and flavour with the lemon juice.

* Blend the egg mixture with the combined cream and curd cheese, and add a little sugar to taste, if desired. The mixture should have a refreshing tang.

* Heat the fruit sauce or puréed, stewed fruit to approx. 50°C. Stir in the rest of the gelatine and the thawed bilberries.

* Remove the cake from the oven paper, divide it into two equal halves and cover one half with the mixture of cream and curd cheese. Place the other half on top, and garnish with the bilberries and fruit sauce or stewed fruit.
* Leave the cake to cool. Trim the sides before serving, and divide the cake into portions.

Mediterranean lettuces
before loading.

Blue-mould cheeseburger
with celery and walnuts

If the burger is intended as part of a menu comprising several courses, it should be made smaller than the one presented here. The 'bread' is made out of puff-pastry dough and the filling is a version of Waldorf salad with celery and walnuts.

BREAD
2 slices puff-pastry dough
1 egg yolk for brushing
1 tsp sesame seeds

FILLING
1 stalk celery, shredded
50 g walnuts
4 tbs crème fraîche
1 tsp lemon juice
salt, pepper and sugar to taste

ACCOMPANIMENTS
4–8 slices matured blue-
  mould cheese
  (e.g. Roquefort)
4 sticks celery
12 walnuts, toasted

* Cut four rounds of puff-pastry dough and lay them on oven paper. Brush with beaten egg and sprinkle a few sesame seeds on top.
* Bake in an oven preheated to 200°C for approx. 10 minutes or until the dough rises and turns golden brown. Leave to cool on the baking rack.

* Chop the walnuts for the filling and mix with finely shredded celery and crème fraîche. Season to taste with lemon, salt, pepper and a pinch of sugar.
* Cut open the 'rolls', apportion the filling fairly, place the cheese on top with a stick of celery and replace the top halves.

* Decorate with walnuts, toasted in a dry pan, just before serving.

A brasserie should be an informal, cheerful place — and that's what Kastanjen is like.

Marinated steak with fennel chutney
and cold white-pepper sauce

Ordinary beef steaks often tend to turn out somewhat dry and dull, especially if all the fat has been removed. To enhance both flavour and succulence, Bröderna Dahlbom marinate the steaks — thinly sliced — after frying. This makes them more tender, too. The white-pepper sauce with honey and the fennel chutney are perfect accompaniments.

* Fry the steaks in a little butter. Remove from the pan and slice as thinly as possible. Stir together the ingredients for the marinade and marinate the meat for a while — the longer, the richer the flavour.

* Simmer the chopped onion with diced courgettes in a little oil without browning. Add the fennel, also diced, and the sugar, vinegar and salt. Simmer until thick and creamy,

approx. 15–20 minutes. Set aside to cool.

* Mix the ingredients for the white-pepper sauce until smooth.

* Boil the pasta, leave to cool and mix with finely chopped leek.
* Divide the meat between four plates, put a little leek-pasta mixture on top, pour on the white-pepper sauce and finish off with a dollop of chutney.

What a performance!
The kitchen as a stage
and the meal as a drama,
starring the cooks,
at Bröderna Dahlbom.

STEAKS
4 beef steaks (e.g. fillet),
　approx. 120 g each
butter for frying
1 dl soy sauce
2 dl chili sauce
1 dl water
1 onion, chopped

CHUTNEY
1 onion, chopped
oil for frying
500 g fennel, diced
300 g courgettes, diced
2 dl sugar
1 1/2 dl white-wine vinegar
2 tsp salt

PEPPER SAUCE
2 dl crème fraîche
1 heaped tbs honey
15 white peppercorns, ground
1 1/2–2 tbs water

ACCOMPANIMENTS
pasta
finely chopped leek

Dill carrots with salt herring and sour lemon cream

The 'crowns' — flowering heads or umbels — of dill make a very strong seasoning, commonly used for cooking crayfish and making various kinds of pickled herring. This dish should preferably be made from carrots grown in outdoor soil, flavoured with fresh dill umbels or dill seed.

CARROTS
4–5 peeled carrots
  (300–400 g)
2 tbs dill seed (or umbels
  in season)
2 tbs olive oil
salt and pepper to taste

HERRING
2 large herring fillets,
  salted and soaked

CREAM
1 1/2–2 dl sour cream
grated rind of 1/2 lemon

* Cut the carrots in centimetre-thick slices. Place a saucepan over medium heat, pour in the oil and add the carrots and dill.
* Simmer gently under a lid until tender, but without browning.
* Season to taste with salt and pepper.

* Mix the sour cream with the grated lemon rind.
* Cut the herring into attractive pieces. Dish up on individual plates or a large dish as a cold hors d'œuvre or light lunch dish. Freshly boiled potatoes make a suitable accompaniment.

Petri Pumpa ranks among Sweden's very best restaurants.

Herb-marinated prawns
with chopped eggs and orange vinaigrette

PRAWNS
400 g prawns, boiled and
  shelled

HERB MARINADE
1 tbs white-wine vinegar
4 tbs oil
1/4 tsp white pepper,
  freshly ground
1 tbs tarragon, chopped
1 tbs chives, chopped
1 tbs thyme, chopped

EGGS
4 eggs, hard-boiled
4 tbs sunflower seeds
1 red onion, finely chopped
approx. 10 cm cucumber,
  peeled

VINAIGRETTE
1/2 dl orange juice,
  freshly squeezed
rind of 2 oranges,
  finely grated
1/2 tbs white-wine vinegar
1 dl oil
1/2 tbs sugar
salt to taste

Scandinavians tend to eat fresh, boiled prawns *au naturel*. Here, however, they are served with eggs and onions – classic herring accompaniments – plus a vinaigrette made of orange juice. To make the dish as pretty as in the picture, use a mould without a base and remove it just before serving.

* Mix the ingredients for the herb marinade and add the shelled prawns.
* Chop the hard-boiled eggs and mix with the sunflower seeds, finely chopped onion and cucumber cut into tiny cubes.

* Stir together the orange vinaigrette and season with salt to taste.

* Shape the chopped-egg mixture into upright cylinders on four plates, lay the prawns on top and drip the orange vinaigrette around the food.
* Fresh herbs make a suitable garnish.

Bröderna Dahlbom in Gothenburg has achieved tremendous success with its inspired cross-cooking.

Poached spring onion with goat's cheese and black sesame seeds in a sweet dressing

Norway is known for its fine goat's cheeses, and Sweden and Denmark above all for their hard cheeses, such as *Västerbotten* and *Havarti* respectively. Today there is a flourishing market for new, small cheese producers, who often concentrate on fine white ewe's-milk and goat's cheeses. This elegant dish should preferably be made from one of these, but Greek *feta* cheese is an acceptable alternative.

✳ Rinse the spring onions well to remove all the sand and soil. Cut them up and simmer in lightly salted water for a few minutes. The onions should retain their firmness. Then cool them in cold water, and drain on kitchen paper.
✳ Dice the goat's cheese and roll it in sesame seeds. Lay the dice on the spring onions and sprinkle salt and pepper on top.
✳ Melt the honey, whisk in the vinegar and oil, and season with salt and pepper to taste. Drip the dressing over the cheese and serve.

Thomas Drejing has mastered the art of bringing out and accentuating flavours.

ONION AND CHEESE
250–300 g spring onions
  (or young leeks)
150 g white goat's cheese
  (or *feta*)
1 tbs black sesame seeds
salt and pepper

DRESSING
1 dl olive oil
1/2 tbs honey
2 tbs white-wine vinegar
salt and pepper

MENU
No. 3

By ANDERS LAURING
Brasserie Kastanjen

✳

Crayfish soup
with fresh chervil

Quail with polenta,
mushroom and
thyme-flavoured gravy

Caramelised pineapple
with coconut sorbet

✳

RECIPES ON PAGES 74–76

Crayfish soup with fresh chervil

A superb soup is the commencement to this meal. Before serving, mix it in the blender with lightly whipped cream. The frothy soup is then served in a large, warmed dish, garnished with a few shelled crayfish.

SOUP
Shells and remains of 20
 cleaned crayfish
oil for browning
2 tbs tomato purée
5 dl veal stock
5 dl white wine
5 dl fish stock (or water)
1 onion, coarsely chopped
1/4 celeriac, coarsely
 chopped
1 leek, sliced
1 tsp coriander seeds
2 sprigs from fresh dill umbels
 (or dill seeds)
salt, pepper, more tomato
 purée if desired
cayenne pepper to taste

ACCOMPANIMENTS
20 crayfish
2 dl whipped cream
1 bunch chervil

* Shell and clean the crayfish. Set them aside, and chop up the shells. Prepare and cut up the vegetables.
* Heat up the oil in a large saucepan and toss in the crayfish shells and

remains. Add the vegetables and sauté them as well. Then add the tomato purée and coriander seeds, and pour in the veal stock, wine and water or fish stock.
* Bring to the boil and simmer gently for approx. 30 minutes, skimming thoroughly from time to time.
* Remove the saucepan from the heat and leave to stand for approx. 30 minutes. Then strain the soup and carry on simmering until it is reduced to some 8–10 decilitres.
* Season the soup with a pinch of cayenne pepper, salt and freshly ground pepper.

* Whip the cream until frothy, but not too thick. Just before serving, mix half the cream with the soup and then spoon the other half on top as decoration.

* Heat the crayfish in a hot pan and lay them in the soup. Garnish with fresh chervil or a sprig of dill.

Quail with polenta, mushroom and thyme-flavoured gravy

Polenta has become ever more popular. The maize grains are available in different degrees of fineness; here, the Polenta Express variety is used. The flavour of the maize can be further enhanced with a little sweetcorn purée if so desired. With it, one or two quail are served per portion, depending on the birds' size.

* Bring the water for the polenta to the boil and add a small amount of salt. Whisk in the polenta a little at a time. Whisk thoroughly to blend well.
* Simmer the polenta gently for 5–6 minutes while whisking vigorously. The polenta should form a fairly thick porridge.
* Stir in the Parmesan (and the sweetcorn purée if desired).

* Season the quail with salt and white pepper.
* Heat up the oil in a casserole or pan and brown the birds with thyme and garlic.
* Put the quail in a roasting pan and place them in the oven for 5 minutes at 175°C.
* Remove the birds from the oven and cover with foil. Set aside until serving. Carve immediately before dishing them up.

* Skim off the fat and strain the gravy. Pour in the wine and chicken stock. Simmer for a couple of minutes.
* Strain the stock and reduce it to 2–3 decilitres. Season with salt and pepper to taste. Stir in a dab of butter before serving.

* Fry the chanterelles in butter with chopped garlic for a few minutes.
* Shape the polenta attractively on hot plates. This is most easily done using an open mould.
* Dish up the quail surrounded by mushrooms and thyme gravy.

QUAIL
4 large or 8 small quail,
   ready for cooking
olive oil for browning
2 sprigs of thyme
6 whole garlic cloves

THYME-FLAVOURED GRAVY
Gravy from the quail
1 dl white wine
3 dl chicken stock
salt and pepper to taste
finely chopped thyme
1 tbs butter

POLENTA
1 1/2 dl polenta (Express)
6 dl water + salt
2 tbs butter
1 tbs grated Parmesan
(2 tbs sweetcorn purée
   if desired)

ACCOMPANIMENTS
300 g small chanterelles
   and/or mushrooms
1/2 garlic clove, finely chopped
butter for frying

Caramelised pineapple
with coconut sorbet

A pleasing dessert that can be prepared well ahead. Start with the sorbet, since it takes about 5 hours to freeze. To garnish, use dried pineapple chips and strands of caramelised sugar.

PINEAPPLE
2 fresh pineapples

CARAMEL
1 dl pineapple juice
2 dl sugar

SORBET
2 dl coconut purée (available in tins)
1 dl syrup (1 dl water + 50 g sugar)
1 tbs glucose

CHIPS
12 thin slices pineapple
oil for brushing
1 tbs sugar

* Boil the water and sugar for the syrup. Add the coconut purée and glucose and simmer until the glucose has melted.
* Chill and run the sorbet in an ice-cream machine until the desired hardness is achieved, or pour the mixture into a bowl and place it in the freezer. When the sorbet mixture is half-frozen remove it and run it in a blender, after which it should be returned to the freezer until frozen through, which takes 4–5 hours.

* Peel the pineapples and cut them into a shape resembling a straight-sided tea caddy. Cut out as many thin slices as you need for the chips (about half a pineapple).
* Lay the thin slices on greased and lightly sugared oven paper and dry in an oven at 100°C for approx. 45 minutes. Leave the chips to stand in a dry place.

* Cut the rest of the pineapples into slices approx. 1 cm thick and lay them on a greased grilling rack to make a pleasing grid pattern. Leave to cool on oven paper.

* Boil the sugar and pineapple juice for a few minutes until the mixture is slightly caramelised. Put in the pineapple slices and simmer for 2–3 minutes. Remove the slices and brush them with the hot caramel.
* Keep simmering the caramel, testing it now and again by pouring a little onto a cold plate. When it sets it is ready: the caramel may be drawn out in strands that, when they set, can decorate the dessert.

* Build a big 'egg' with the coconut sorbet on the pineapple slices, and decorate with the chips and caramel.

Making fresh spätzle
is a great art.

COD
600 g cod fillet (4 pieces,
  150 g each) with skin
1/2 dl olive oil
salt and pepper to taste

SAUERKRAUT
1 head of cabbage
2 dl white-wine vinegar
1 tbs sugar
2 tbs salt
6 dl white wine
2 onions, chopped
200 g bacon, in one piece
1/4 tsp caraway seeds
5 dl light veal stock (or other
  meat stock)
salt and white pepper to taste
1 tbs butter

RED-WINE SAUCE
5 shallots
2 garlic cloves
1/4 tsp black peppercorns
1 bay leaf
6 dl red wine
3 dl port
1 tbs raisins
5 dl dark veal stock (or other
  meat stock)
2 tbs butter
salt and pepper to taste

ACCOMPANIMENTS
80 g beef marrow
1 tbs chives, finely chopped

Baked North Sea cod with sauerkraut, grilled bacon, red-wine sauce and beef marrow

Cod is a choice North Sea delicacy. Here, it is baked gently and served with sauerkraut and a tasty red-wine sauce – a trifle unorthodox, but singularly successful. It takes about six to eight weeks to make sauerkraut, but you can always buy it ready-made.

* Remove the cabbage stem and cut the leaves into shreds 1/2 centimetre wide.
* Put the shredded cabbage in a mixing bowl, pour in the white-wine vinegar, sugar and salt and mix thoroughly.
* Cover with plastic foil, place a heavy weight on top and leave in a cool place for 6–8 weeks.

* Rinse the cabbage and place it in a saucepan. Pour in the white wine and veal stock, add the chopped onion and bacon, season with caraway seeds and simmer for two hours. The cabbage should be soft but still elastic.
* When the cabbage is cooked, remove the bacon (to grill just before serving).
* Season the sauerkraut with salt and white pepper and keep it hot. Round off with a dab of butter, if desired, before serving.

* Peel and slice the shallots and garlic thinly and toast in a saucepan with black pepper and bay leaves. Pour in the red wine, port and dark veal stock, and add the raisins.
* Reduce the sauce to one-third and season with salt and pepper. Strain the sauce through a fine sieve, dot a little butter on top and keep it warm.

* Rub the cod with salt, pepper and olive oil. Bake at a low temperature, 120°C, for approx. 8–10 minutes.

* Slice the beef marrow and put it in the residual (i.e. low) heat of the oven to warm for approx. 3 minutes.
* Cut the bacon into four largish slices and grill them on both sides, so that they take on an attractive grid pattern.
* Put a generous pile of sauerkraut on four large, warmed plates. Place the cod on the sauerkraut, lay a piece of beef marrow on each one and sprinkle with chives. Pour sauce around the food and garnish with the bacon.

Potato terrine with marinated onion and grilled fish

The fish or meat can be left out of many Erwin Lauterbach recipes. They are thus a treasure trove for vegetarians. This potato terrine is, in fact, scrumptious in its own right. The onion, too, can be served solo, hot or cold, preferably with grated Parmesan on top.

* Peel the onions and boil them until soft in lightly salted water. Remove the onions from the water, drain and lay them in a bowl. Sprinkle with the olives and tarragon.
* Whisk together the marinade ingredients, season to taste and then pour it over the hot onions. Leave to stand for an hour or so.

* Peel the potatoes and slice them thinly. Boil in lightly salted water for approx. 2 minutes.
* Grease a long bread tin with butter or put greased paper in the bottom of the tin.

* Bring to the boil 1 decilitre of cream and season with salt, pepper and a little garlic.
* Beat the eggs with 1 decilitre of grated cheese and the rest of the cream. Add the hot cream. Season with salt and pepper if necessary.

* Stir the sliced potato into the egg mixture so that the slices are covered. Spoon out the potato and place a layer on the bottom of the tin. Pour in more egg mixture, sprinkle cheese and a little tarragon on top, and continue alternating the potato, cheese and tarragon, finishing with a layer of potato.
* Bake the terrine in a bain-marie for about 45 minutes to 1 hour at 175°C, until the potatoes are cooked and the terrine is firm in consistency. Cover the tin with foil if it is becoming too brown.

* Leave the terrine to cool slightly before detaching it from the tin. Cut as many slices as you expect will be needed.
* Serve with onions and a grilled fish fillet; pike perch or ocean perch are suitable accompaniments. Grill the fish, skin side up, for approx. 3 minutes. Dish up the fish, still with the skin side up. Season with salt and pepper, and garnish with lettuce.

POTATO TERRINE

1 kg medium-sized potatoes
4 eggs
1 1/2 dl grated Emmenthal cheese
3 dl whipping cream
3 tbs butter
2 tbs finely chopped tarragon
2 garlic cloves, pressed
salt and pepper

ONIONS

16–20 pearl onions or small yellow-skinned onions
water and salt
1 tbs black olives, chopped
1 tsp tarragon, chopped

MARINADE

2 dl olive oil
1 dl balsam vinegar
2 tsp Chinese soy sauce
salt and freshly ground white pepper
1 clove garlic, pressed

ACCOMPANIMENTS

4 fish fillets with skin, e.g. pike perch or ocean perch
salt and pepper
4 lettuce leaves

Grilled tuna with potato and wasabi purée and soy gravy

A Japanese-inspired dish in which *wasabi* (green Japanese horse-radish), tuna and soy sauce are the primary ingredients. Ginger and sesame seeds accentuate its oriental character.

* Start by peeling and boiling the potatoes, then mash them and stir in enough boiling milk to make the consistency right: it should be fairly stiff. Season with wasabi (carefully, it has a dominant flavour). Add salt and pepper, and stir in a little butter before serving.

* Simmer finely chopped garlic in the sherry and the two soy sauces. Grate a little ginger into the pan and season with sesame oil. Sprinkle with sesame seeds before serving.

* Cut the leek into long, wide shreds. Rinse them thoroughly and boil them for a minute or so in lightly salted water.
* Pour off the water and add butter, along with finely chopped chives.
* Pick up a quarter of the leek ribbons using long tweezers, so that they hang over one side, and wind them into spools in the hollow of your hand.

* Extract the tweezers and place the spools upright on warmed plates.
* Do the same with the rest of the leek.

* Dish up the grilled tuna beside the mashed potatoes and pour the soy gravy on top.

FISH
4 pieces tuna, 150 g each
salt, pepper and freshly ground coriander
oil for frying

POTATO PURÉE
8 potatoes
1–2 dl milk, boiling
wasabi (preferably in powder form, but also available in tubes)
salt and pepper
2 tbs butter

SOY GRAVY
2 cloves garlic, finely chopped
1 dl sherry
1/2 dl water
1/2 dl Japanese soy sauce (salty)
1/2 dl Chinese soy sauce (sweet)
fresh ginger, grated
1/2 tbs sesame seeds
1–2 tbs sesame oil

ACCOMPANIMENTS
2 leeks
water and salt
2 tbs butter
2 tbs finely chopped chives

Venison medallions with chanterelle sauce and potato pancakes

Venison, especially from fallow deer, is delicious. One rule is that the better cuts, including the fillets, must never be well done. Chanterelles are a prized delicacy that, in some years, may be found in such profusion as to give a golden lustre to the Scandinavian forest floor. Potato pancakes are a Swedish classic.

VENISON
600 g fillet of venison
salt and pepper
butter for frying

CHANTERELLE SAUCE
200 g chanterelles, cleaned,
  in pieces
butter for frying
1 onion, finely chopped
2 dl whipping cream
salt and pepper
1 tbs port

POTATO PANCAKES
8 large potatoes, coarsely
  grated
1/2 leek, finely chopped
butter and oil for frying

ACCOMPANIMENT
cherry tomatoes

* Sauté the onion in a little butter without browning. Add the chanterelles and fry everything over medium heat until the chanterelles have shrunk. Pour in the cream and braise the chanterelles gently until the sauce has reached a suitably thick consistency.
* Season with salt, pepper and port.

* Peel the potatoes and grate them on the coarse side of the grater.
* Rinse the leek well and finely chop up some of the green part.
* Mix the leek into the grated potatoes, season with salt and pepper, and fry small pancakes in equal quantities of butter and oil.

* Cut the venison fillet into four thick slices. Sprinkle salt and pepper on the meat and fry it over medium heat. The meat should be pinkish inside.

* Serve the venison fillet with mushroom sauce and the newly fried potato pancakes. Garnish the plates with cherry tomatoes.

MENU
No. 4

By THOMAS DREJING
Petri Pumpa

✳

Poached breast of cockercl
with celeriac-anchovy ragout

Fennel-steamed Naiad
salmon with almond potatoes
and thyme

Lingonberry and chocolate
cream on a nut base

✳

RECIPES ON PAGES 88–90

Poached breast of cockerel
with celeriac-anchovy ragout

Sweden has rightly become famous for its fine, healthy poultry. This cockerel comes from Raskarum in Skåne (Scania), Sweden's southernmost province, and weighs over 2 kilograms. The carcase can be used to make stock in which the breasts are then simmered. Celeriac and anchovy provide robust complementary flavours.

MEAT

750–800 g cockerel breasts

STOCK

1 1/2 litres water
cockerel carcase
1 carrot, in pieces
celeriac peel etc. (see below)
parsley stalks
1 garlic clove
5 white peppercorns
a little salt

RAGOUT

250–300 g celeriac,
  coarsely diced
50 g anchovies, finely chopped
1 dl whipping cream
1 tbs lemon juice
1 bunch parsley, coarsely
  chopped
salt or pepper to taste

* Scrub the celeriac until clean, peel it, cut it into large cubes and simmer them in lightly salted water until soft. Strain in a sieve.
* Divide the cockerel carcase in pieces and bring to the boil in water. Skim and add the carrot, garlic and parsley stalks with the peel and other discarded parts of the celeriac. Season. Simmer for 30 minutes. Strain.
* Simmer the cockerel breasts in stock for approx. 10–15 min.
* Take the saucepan off the heat and put it aside for 5–10 minutes. This time depends on the thickness of the cockerel breasts: pierce with a skewer and check that the meat juice is pale and transparent.

* Whip the cream until semi-stiff and add the anchovies, lemon juice and coarsely chopped parsley. Add the diced celeriac. Mix, and season with salt and pepper to taste.

* Cut the cockerel breasts lengthwise. On each plate, arrange three slices of breast around the celeriac-anchovy ragout.

Fennel-steamed Naiad salmon with almond potatoes and thyme

'Naiad salmon' is a Swedish speciality made by first sugar-salting and then cold-smoking the salmon to impart a mild, delicate flavour and attractive colour. Here, it is then steamed on a bed of fennel and thyme and then served hot with 'almond potatoes', a unique Swedish variety with a slightly nutty taste.

* Sauté the shallot in oil for a few minutes. Pour the white wine on top and simmer together until reduced to half.
* Add the fish stock and put in the fennel, sliced, with a few sprigs of thyme. Cover and steam until the fennel is tender.
* Boil and peel the almond potatoes and cut them into large pieces. Add the potatoes to the fennel in the saucepan. Shake the pan to mix everything, and season with salt and pepper to taste.
* Cut the salmon into four pieces, lay them on the bed of fennel, cover and steam the fish for a couple of minutes.
* Serve the fish, fennel and potatoes in equal portions on four warmed plates. Garnish with fresh thyme.

Tired after your meal? Petri Pumpa runs a hotel on the first floor.

SALMON
600–700 g Naiad salmon, boned fillets
1 shallot, finely chopped
2 tbs olive oil
1 dl white wine
1 dl fish stock, from cube
2 heads of fennel, in slices 1/2 cm thick
250 g almond potatoes
thyme
salt and pepper to taste

ACCOMPANIMENT
fresh thyme

Lingonberry and chocolate cream on a nut base

The Scandinavian fruit known as the 'lingonberry' is something entirely out of the ordinary. Replete with vitamin C and refreshingly sharp, it is a classic accompaniment to many popular everyday Swedish dishes. The berries have sugar stirred in when raw, or are boiled with sugar, for the flavour's sake. They contain their own preservative.

NUT BASES
1 dl egg whites
100 g sugar
130 g hazelnuts, ground

LINGONBERRY CREAM
2 dl sweetened raw
  lingonberries
300 g milk chocolate
  (for cooking)
2 dl whipping cream

ACCOMPANIMENT
2 dl sweetened raw lingonberries, mixed in blender
  and strained

* Whip the egg whites until stiff. Add the sugar and continue whisking as for meringue.
* Fold in the finely ground hazelnuts.
* Spread out the mixture on oven paper, in two equal-sized bases.
* Bake at 200°c for 5–10 minutes, until the nut bases have turned golden brown.
* They can either be sandwiched together with the lingonberry cream to make a single large 'cake', or cut into small triangles, circles, etc., according to one's imagination and wishes.

* Mix the lingonberries in the blender until smoothly puréed.
* Melt the chocolate in a bain-marie or the microwave and mix it with the lingonberries.
* Whip the cream lightly and stir it in the lingonberry cream with firm, vigorous movements.
* Spread the cream between the nut bases, and chill for a few hours.

* Serve with lingonberry sauce made with sweetened raw lingonberries, mixed in the blender and strained through a sieve.

A modern version of a classic table setting at Petri Pumpa, where the aesthetic aspects of eating out are taken seriously.

Roulades of witch flounder with vegetable couscous and lemon sauce

The North African speciality couscous is increasingly cropping up in casseroles all over the world. Here, the small grains are mixed with vegetables and red onion, and served with steamed witch flounder (also known as 'pole flounder'). A sharp lemon sauce is a suitable accompaniment.

FISH
600–700 g fillets of witch flounder
120 g plain cream cheese (e.g. Philadelphia)
fresh tarragon
salt and pepper to taste

COUSCOUS
500 g couscous
5 dl water
juice of 1 lemon
olive oil
salt to taste
2 tomatoes
1 yellow sweet pepper
1 red onion

SAUCE
juice and grated rind of 1 lemon
1 tbs honey
8 tbs crème fraîche
1 tbs water
salt to taste

ACCOMPANIMENT
1 lemon

* Beat the cream cheese until smooth, spread it on the flounder fillets and sprinkle with finely chopped tarragon. Add salt and pepper, and roll up the fillets.
* Lay the rolled fillets in an oven dish in a few centimetres of water and bake at 175°c for approx. 10 minutes. The cooking time may vary according to the thickness of the fillets.

* Bring the water, flavoured with the lemon juice, a little olive oil and salt, to the boil. Put the couscous in a bowl, pour in the hot water and stir. Leave to swell for approx. 10 minutes.
* Finely chop the tomatoes, pepper and red onion, and mix with the couscous. Season with salt and pepper.

* Stir together the ingredients for the lemon sauce and season with salt to taste.

* Divide the fish rolls between 4 plates and place the couscous on one side and a dollop of lemon sauce on the other. Garnish with elegantly sliced lemon.

Anders Dahlbom – like his younger brother Jonas – has won the title of 'Cook of the year' in Sweden.

Knuckle of veal in oyster and mushroom fricassee

Back in the Middle Ages, oysters were already a delicacy prized by the Scandinavian aristocracy, who preferred to eat them cooked in one form or another, such as sauce. Here, with the marrow from the knuckle of veal, the oysters are gently heated in a little stock before joining the mushrooms on the plate or in the casserole.

* Pick the marrow out of the shaft of the knuckle bone. Put the marrow in cold water.

* Then boil the knuckle with the vegetables in enough water to cover. Bring to the boil, skim well and then add the seasoning.

* Simmer gently until the meat is tender, which takes 30–50 minutes depending on the quality of the meat.

* Strain the stock and reduce to approx. 3 decilitres.

* Sweat the shallots and garlic in the butter. Add the cleaned fungi, season with lemon rind and finely shredded tarragon in the saucepan and stir.

* Pour on 2 decilitres of the veal stock and the juice from the freshly opened oysters. Simmer gently under a lid for approx. 5 minutes.

* Season to taste with salt, pepper and a little more coarsely chopped tarragon.

* Heat the remaining veal stock and slide the oysters gently into it with the marrow. They should be given only a modicum of heat, and then mixed into the fricassee immediately before serving.

VEAL
600 g knuckle of veal, in slices 2 cm thick
1/2 carrot
1/2 leek
1/4 celeriac
parsley and tarragon stalks
2 bay leaves
1 sprig of thyme
6 white peppercorns
1 tsp salt
water to cover

FRICASSEE
1 shallot, finely chopped
2 garlic cloves, finely chopped
1 tbs butter
1 sprig of tarragon, shredded
grated rind of 1/2 lemon
1/2 litre mixed fungi, in pieces
2 dl veal stock (from the knuckle)
4–12 freshly opened oysters + juice
salt and pepper

Veal brisket with dark gravy and mashed potato

This is classic Scandinavian everyday fare at its best. After prolonged boiling, the meat becomes remarkably tender. Leave the cartilage: it imparts a fine flavour and makes good jelly. Boil the veal brisket the day before serving, and chill under pressure. Carve attractively to serve.

* Boil the veal brisket with the cleaned vegetables, and preferably use the discarded parts (brushed clean) of celeriac and carrot, and also the onion skin, to give an extra boost to the flavour. Salt lightly and simmer for 1 1/2–2 hours.
* Remove the meat from the stock and set aside to cool before transferring it to a narrow container. Pour on the sieved stock, put a cloth over the container and a light weight on top, and refrigerate the veal overnight.

* Brown the coarsely chopped onion and celeriac in olive oil until almost burnt. Add the rosemary and pour in the sieved veal stock, but save a little to heat the meat in. Reduce to about one-quarter. By this time the gravy has a tasty flavour. If, like Lauterbach, you prefer a richer and more concentrated gravy sauce, continue until the sauce is reduced to approx. 2 decilitres.
* Strain the gravy and stir in 1 table-spoonful of butter just before serving.

* Boil and mash the potatoes and work in the olive oil, perhaps mixed with grape oil if the olive flavour is too dominant. Dilute with potato broth to the desired consistency. Season to taste with salt and pepper.

* Peel and blanch the garlic cloves 5–6 times, straining them and discarding the water each time. This gives the garlic a subtle and slightly sweetish flavour.
* Heat up a little oil in a pan and sauté the pearl onions until soft. Then add the garlic cloves and black olives.

* Cut the meat into even slices and heat it gently in the saved veal stock. Serve the meat on warmed plates with mashed potato, sprinkled with a little grated lemon rind. Garnish with the olives, pearl onions and garlic. Pour the gravy sauce on top.

MEAT
2 kg veal brisket (thicker part)
1 onion
cloves
1 leek
1/4 celeriac
1 carrot
1 tsp salt
water

GRAVY SAUCE
veal stock (liquid from cooking)
2 onions
1/4 celeriac
1 sprig of rosemary
2 tbs oil
2 tbs butter

MASHED POTATO
1 kg potato
1 dl olive oil + potato broth
salt and pepper to taste
grated lemon rind

ACCOMPANIMENTS
1/2 celeriac, finely diced
14–16 pearl onions
20 garlic cloves
1 dl small black olives
2 tbs olive oil

MENU
No. 5

By EYVIND HELLSTRØM
Bagatelle

Scampi in their shells with
white-wine sauce

Saddle of fallow deer with
pears and spinach

Apple charlotte with
caramel sauce
and candied orange peel

RECIPES ON PAGES 100–102

Scampi in their shells with white-wine sauce

The scampi in this hors d'œuvre must be raw: if they are precooked, part of their flavour is already lost. This, of course, means that they must be — if not alive — absolutely freshly caught. This goes virtually without saying in Scandinavia, with the proximity of rich fishing waters.

SCAMPI

16 scampi
1/2 head of lettuce
1/2 red sweet pepper
1/2 yellow sweet pepper
butter
salt and pepper to taste

SAUCE

1 dl white wine
1 shallot, finely chopped
1 tbs cold water
200 g butter, unsalted
1–2 sprigs of tarragon
1 tbs whipped cream

ACCOMPANIMENTS

mixed varieties of lettuce
vinaigrette

* Cut the scampi lengthwise and remove the intestines.
* Poach the lettuce leaves in salted water until soft. Strain and chill in cold water.
* Divide the sweet peppers and cut out the flesh. Cut out small stars with a cutter, or dice the sweet peppers.

* Melt a little butter in a pan and sauté the pieces of sweet pepper for a few minutes without browning.
* Lay a row of salad on each scampi and decorate with the red and yellow sweet pepper.
* This can be prepared well ahead.

* Chop the shallot and a sprig of tarragon. Place the shallot and tarragon in a saucepan and pour in the wine. Simmer until 1 tablespoonful remains. Add water.
* Dice the butter finely and stir it gradually into the reduced liquid.

* Season the sauce to taste, strain it and add a little finely chopped tarragon.

* Place the scampi in a dry, hot pan with the shell side down and brown for approx. 5 minutes.
* Fold a spoonful of whipped cream into the sauce to make it light and frothy.
* Serve the browned scampi straight from the pan with white-wine sauce, and sprinkle a little salt over each. A bouquet of salad, tossed in a light vinaigrette, is served alongside each portion.

Saddle of fallow deer
with pears and spinach

The Scandinavian forests offer abundant game, both big and small, and venison is a major tradition. Fallow deer is Eyvind Hellstrøm's favourite meat. Here, it comes from a newly shot animal kept in captivity in eastern Norway. The meat is then hung for approx. 12 days in Bagatelle's cellar to make it tender.

* Cut out both fillets on either side of the saddle. Set aside for the time being.

* Hack the bones to pieces and brown in equal quantities of butter and oil.
* Clean and trim the vegetables. Cut up and brown with the bones.
* Transfer everything to a casserole and pour in red wine and water to cover. Bring to the boil, skim and continue boiling until the liquid has almost all evaporated. Add water and boil for another hour.
* Peel the pears and cut them into segments. Trim them into attractive shapes.
* Strain the stock and add the discarded pieces of pear. Boil the stock until reduced to half (approx. 2 dl).
* Blend the stock with a dab of butter.

* Fry the pear segments in butter with a little sugar for approx. 5 minutes, until they are an attractive golden brown.

Sprinkle the liquorice powder on top and shake the pan to mix everything thoroughly. Keep the pears warm.

* Place the well-rinsed spinach in a saucepan with a little butter in the bottom. When the spinach is steamed through, spear a clove of garlic on a fork and stir the spinach with it to impart an intriguing hint of garlic. Flavour with a pinch of sugar and a modicum of salt. Discard the garlic.

* Heat up butter and/or oil in a frying pan, crush the juniper berries and add them with the thyme and peeled cloves of a whole garlic. Stir, and lay the whole fallow-deer fillets in the pan. Season with salt and pepper, and brown the meat on all sides over medium heat. Continue frying the meat for approx. 5 minutes. Set aside for 5 minutes before cutting up the fillets.

MEAT
1 double saddle of
  fallow deer
butter and oil for frying
4 crushed juniper berries
1 sprig of thyme
1 whole garlic
salt and pepper

SAUCE
bones from the saddle
1 carrot
1 onion
1 garlic clove
1 piece of celeriac
Sichuan pepper
1/2 bottle of red wine
water

SPINACH
120–150 g fresh spinach
1 tbs butter
1 garlic clove
1/2 tsp sugar
1/2 tsp salt

ACCOMPANIMENTS
4 Williams pears
butter for frying
1 tsp sugar
1 tsp liquorice powder
  (available at chemist's)
cranberries
butter and sugar for frying

Apple charlotte with caramel sauce and candied orange peel

This charlotte is prepared the day before serving: it needs 7 hours in the oven to liquefy properly. The juice that collects is served as an accompaniment, as are candied orange peel and a dollop of whipped cream. The quantities are estimated for 6–8 people.

APPLES
10 apples (Granny Smith)
100 g sugar

CARAMEL SAUCE
100 g sugar
2 dl water

ORANGE
peel of 1 orange
100 g sugar
1 dl water

ACCOMPANIMENTS
apple-caramel sauce
mint leaves
lightly whipped cream

* Boil the sugar and water to make a syrup.
* Use a soufflé dish that holds 1 1/2 litres. Cover the bottom and sides with the syrup.

* Peel the apples and remove the cores. Cut the apples into very thin slices and place one layer of slices in the bottom of the dish. Sprinkle sugar over them and then put another layer of apple slices, turned in the other direction, on top.
* Fill the dish with apple slices and sugar in alternating layers, and continue with a few more layers until the filling reaches 5 centimetres (2 inches) above the edge of the dish.
* Cover the dish with aluminium foil with a few air holes pricked in it.
* Place the dish of apples in a bain-marie and put it in the oven at 180°C. Leave for 7 hours until the apples have fused and liquefied. Set the charlotte aside to cool and pour off the juice from the apples into a bowl.

* Shred the orange peel, excluding the white pith. Lay the shredded peel in a saucepan, pour on water and bring rapidly to the boil.
* Pour off the water and add 1 decilitre of fresh water with 100 grams of sugar. Simmer gently for 2 hours, until the peel is caramelised.

* To serve, cut the charlotte into attractive slices (simplest with an electric knife) and serve it with the caramelised shredded orange peel and apple-caramel sauce. Garnish with mint leaves and softly whipped cream around the plate.

Rare 'oldies' on the digestif (liqueur) trolley and new goodies (Bård Breivik) from Galleri Riis on the walls of Bagatelle.

Curry-braised fillet of beef
with lime onions and rice with lentils

When, as here, meat is braised in a casserole with veal stock and seasoning, it becomes extra tender and succulent. How hot a curry powder to choose is a matter of taste. The important thing is to fry it with the meat: then the flavour reaches its full strength.

* Trim the fillet of beef, sprinkle it with salt and pepper, and roll it in curry powder. Brown well on all sides in a casserole.
* Pour on the veal stock (available ready-made) and braise the meat until the desired inner temperature is attained. How long this takes depends both on the degree of heat used and on how well one wants the meat done.
* Remove the meat and put it aside.
* Reduce the stock further, until it has a strong and agreeable flavour.
* Enrich the stock by stirring in the butter before serving.

* Soak the lentils for approx. 1 hour. Remove, mix with the rice and cook them in 5 decilitres of salted water for 20 minutes.

* Peel the onions and brown them in butter.
* Pour in the water, with the lime juice and rind. Season with salt to taste, and simmer the onions until soft.

* Distribute the small onions on four warmed plates. Cut the fillet of beef in four thick slices, and lay them on top of the onion. Put the lentils and rice on one side and pour a little gravy stock around the food. Garnish with chives or blanched scallions.

MEAT
500–600 g fillet of beef
curry powder
5 dl veal stock
1 tbs butter
salt and pepper to taste

ONIONS
20 small onions
butter for frying
juice and grated rind of
  2 limes
1 litre water
salt to taste

RICE
2 dl rice
1/2 dl red and green lentils
5 dl water
salt to taste

ACCOMPANIMENT
chives or thin scallions
  (or spring onions)

Globe artichokes in dill umbels, served with steamed redfish

This modern, low-calorie dish is nonetheless replete with flavour. It can also be served as an entirely vegetarian dish: in that case exclude the fish, and add more vegetables. Here, however, it is served with ocean perch, or redfish as it is also called because of its beautiful rose-red or orange-red colour.

VEGETABLES
4 fleshy globe-artichoke
   hearts
2 sprigs of dill umbel
2 slices of lemon
salt and water
4 parsnips, cut into pieces
4 carrots
2 fennel bulbs, sliced thinly
2 shallots
1/2 sachet saffron (1/4 gram)
salt and pepper to taste
2 tbs olive oil

FISH
4 fish fillets with skin (e.g.
   ocean perch), approx. 150 g
   each
1 tbs olive oil
4 tbs vegetable broth
4 garlic cloves, thinly sliced

ACCOMPANIMENTS
garlic
dill umbels
coriander
lemon
coarse salt

* Clean the vegetables.
* Cut out the artichoke hearts and boil them until soft in water with salt, lemon and a little olive oil. Then trim away any remaining choke or leaves.
* Boil the liquid until reduced to half.

* Pour approx. 2 decilitres of liquid into the bottom of a saucepan and put in the carrots, parsnips in large pieces, dill umbels and thinly sliced fennel bulbs, all at once.
* Sprinkle with saffron, cover with a lid and simmer until the vegetables are soft and hardly any liquid remains.

* Lay the fish fillets in a sauté pan, skin side down. Place the dill, lemon and garlic on top.
* Pour on a little of the artichoke liquid until it just covers the bottom of the pan. Heat gently until the fish is cooked.

* Pour the liquid from the sauté pan into the reduced vegetable broth. Dilute with a little more liquid from the artichoke pan if necessary. The quantity should be approx. 2 decilitres.
* Season with salt, pepper and a little olive oil. Heat up.

* Dish up the fish fillets, skin side up, on warmed plates.
* Lay the vegetables beside the fish and garnish with garlic, lemon, dill and a sprig of fresh coriander. Pour the broth over the vegetables and on the plate.

Pressed knuckle of veal with marinated lentils and oyster fungi

This dish can – or rather, must – be prepared well in advance. The knuckle is first boiled until tender. The meat is then taken off the bone and pressed into a terrine, which must be refrigerated for at least 24 hours. The somewhat Mediterranean-inspired lentils, with their garlic and other seasonings, make a pleasing contrast to the bland meat.

* Put the knuckle of veal in a casserole, pour on water to cover and salt lightly. Add the vegetables and bouquet garni, and simmer gently under a lid.

* When the meat comes away from the bone, it is cooked. Remove the knuckle from the stock and take the remaining meat off the bone.

* Cut the oyster fungi into small pieces and put them in a hot frying pan. Leave over low heat, stirring from time to time. Take off the heat when the fungi have shrunk.

* Cook the lentils in 7 1/2 decilitres of the stock from the meat. Simmer for approx. 20 minutes until soft.

* Add the oyster fungi, vinegar, oil, chopped garlic, salt and pepper.

* Heat the lentils with the chopped vegetables from the veal stock and a bunch of finely chopped chervil, just before serving.

* Boil the veal trimmed from the knuckle with the rest of the stock (approx. 2 litres) from the first cooking, and continue boiling until all the liquid is gone. Season to taste with more salt and pepper. Then press the meat into a mould that holds approx. 1 litre. Cover the mould and refrigerate for 24 hours or so.

* Cut the cucumber into sticks and blanch them in lightly salted water.

* Turn out the terrine, cut it in slices and, if desired, cut out rounds with a cutter (as illustrated).

* Lay a slice of veal terrine on each plate and arrange the lentils, cucumber and a few pieces of oyster fungi around it.

MEAT
1 knuckle (or shin) of veal, approx. 1 kg
1 small carrot
1 small onion
1/8 celeriac
water
1 tsp salt

BOUQUET GARNI
1 sprig of thyme
10 black peppercorns
1 bay leaf
2 garlic cloves
salt and pepper

LENTILS
75 g lentils
7 1/2 dl stock from the meat (see above)
250 g oyster fungi
1/4 dl vinegar
1/2 dl olive oil
1 garlic clove, finely chopped
salt and pepper
1 bunch of chervil, finely chopped
vegetables boiled with the meat (see above)

ACCOMPANIMENTS
cucumber sticks
whole pieces of oyster fungi

Grilled halibut
with basil spätzle and tomato confit

This dish contains many ingenious touches. *Spätzle*, the South German speciality, is made with fresh basil in the dough. And the fish almost cooks itself: just season it with whole white peppercorns and coriander seeds before grilling it on a stripy gridiron.

* Mix the fresh basil and oil in a blender.
* Mix the milk, egg, flour, salt and basil-flavoured oil in a food processor to make a sticky, fairly firm dough. More flour or milk may be needed for the right consistency.
* Lay the dough in a spätzle or purée press with large holes, and press out the dough into boiling, lightly salted water. Be careful not to make too much at once!
* Simmer gently until the spätzle floats up to the surface. Transfer it to ice-cold water with a perforated ladle, to arrest the cooking process.
* Pour away the water and keep the spätzle refrigerated until use.
* Sauté the spätzle rapidly in a frying pan with a little butter, and serve.

* Pack the tomatoes tightly into a saucepan or casserole.
* Pour on enough oil to cover,

and immerse the herbs and garlic.
* Place in an oven preheated to 150°c for approx. 30 minutes, until the tomatoes are soft. Remove them and drain on kitchen paper. The tomatoes should be hot when served — and when cut, their juice trickles out in the form of a delicious and aromatic sauce.

* Season the halibut with salt and freshly ground coriander and white pepper. Lay the fish on a greased gridiron and grill both sides to give it a pleasing pattern. Continue frying the fish gently until it is cooked through and ready for serving.

* Dish up the fried spätzle on hot plates, place the fish on top and arrange the tomatoes around it.

* Coil a little oil flavoured with chili and red sweet pepper around the plate.

FISH
4 slices halibut, approx. 150 g each
salt, pepper and coriander
oil for frying

SPÄTZLE
1 dl olive oil
1/2 pot fresh basil
2 dl milk
2 eggs
approx. 300 g wheat flour
1 tsp salt

TOMATOES
12 ripe tomatoes
4 garlic cloves
fresh thyme, basil and rosemary
oil

ACCOMPANIMENT
oil seasoned with chili and red sweet pepper

Blanquette of chicken
with cabbage and tarragon

Fresh cabbage is an early vegetable that is prized in Scandinavia. Choose the variety that is best for the season; Savoy and white cabbage are suitable for this mild chicken dish, lightly flavoured with lemon and tarragon. To shape the cabbage as elegantly as in the picture, use an open ring mould of an appropriate size.

CHICKEN
4 chicken breasts
1/2 leek
1 piece of celeriac
1 onion
sprigs of parsley
water

SAUCE
2 dl chicken stock (from the
 boiled chicken)
2 egg yolks
2 shallots, finely chopped
1 tbs tarragon, finely chopped
1 dl crème fraîche
juice and grated rind of
 1/2 lemon
salt and pepper to taste

ACCOMPANIMENTS
8 cabbage leaves, blanched
broad-leaved parsley

* Clean the vegetables and cut them up. Bring to the boil the leek, celeriac, onion and a few sprigs of parsley in enough water to cover. Season with salt and add a few peppercorns.
* Boil the vegetables for a while and then add the chicken breasts and simmer gently for approx. 15 minutes, or until the meat is cooked through.

* Remove the chicken breasts and cut them into small pieces.
* Boil the chicken stock with the shallot until reduced to approx. 2 decilitres. Strain it into a small saucepan.
* Whisk in the egg yolks and crème fraîche, and season with lemon, tarragon, salt and pepper.
* Mix the chicken pieces with the sauce and keep hot. NB it must not boil.

* Pull apart the cabbage leaves and blanch them in boiling, salted water until they are soft but still retain their elasticity.
* Remove the leaves and drain them on a cloth. Lay the concave leaves in pairs so as to form small bowls, and fill them with the chicken and sauce. Top with coarsely chopped parsley leaves and serve with boiled potatoes or potato purée.

MENU
No. 6

By ANDERS & JONAS DAHLBOM
Bröderna Dahlbom

Marinated mushroom salad with
sweet-pepper dressing

Smoked halibut
with red-onion vinaigrette

Mango and orange
salad with strawberry caramel
and toffee crisps

RECIPES ON PAGES 116–118

Marinated mushroom salad with sweet-pepper dressing

This attractively coloured dressing, made of red sweet pepper – first oven-baked with a little oil – turns out sweetish but also slightly sour. The dressing can be prepared well in advance, and for added flavour chill the salad for an hour before serving.

SALAD
approx. 16 fresh mushrooms
1/2 red onion,
   finely shredded

DRESSING
2 red sweet peppers
2 tbs oil + oil for baking
1 tbs white-wine vinegar
salt and pepper to taste

ACCOMPANIMENTS
white bread (for croutons)
butter for frying
4 tbs sunflower seeds
cucumber, shredded
red onion, thinly sliced
chives

* Start with the dressing. Divide the peppers and remove the seeds. Rub the halves with a little oil and bake at 175°c for 10 minutes.
* Peel the halved sweet peppers, cut them up and mix them in a blender with the other ingredients. Strain and season with salt and sugar.

* Thinly slice the mushrooms and mix with the thinly sliced red onion. Pour the dressing on top and mix to make a creamy salad, but save a small amount of dressing for garnishing.
* Toss diced white bread in a little butter in a hot pan to make croutons.
* Shape the salad mixture into four neat cylinders: this is easiest using open, round moulds that are lifted away just before serving. Stand a cylinder on each plate and surround it with croutons, diced peppers and sunflower seeds.
* Pour dressing on one side and garnish with the shredded cucumber, red onion and chives.

Smoked halibut
with red-onion vinaigrette

Smoking fish is an old Scandinavian tradition – or rather, preserving method. Here, thin slices of smoked halibut are served in layers alternating with large slices of potatoes boiled in stock, and with vegetables. Serve with a simple vinaigrette.

* Peel the potatoes, cut them into slices approx. 1 centimetre thick and simmer in the stock until soft.
* Divide the slices equally between four plates. Lay the sliced tomatoes, shredded leek and fresh basil on top, followed by a slice of smoked halibut.
* Pour a little vinaigrette on top of each layer. Add another layer of potatoes and vegetables, and finally another slice of fish.

* Pour the last of the vinaigrette around the food and serve.

Oil infusions are typical of Bröderna Dahlbom.

FISH
approx. 500 g halibut
  (120 g/portion)

POTATOES
2 large baking potatoes
5 dl chicken stock

SALAD
2 tomatoes
1 leek, approx. 10 cm long
fresh basil

VINAIGRETTE
1 tbs white-wine vinegar
1 tbs oil
1 red onion, finely chopped
salt and pepper to taste

Mango and orange salad
with strawberry caramel and toffee crisps

The further north you go in Scandinavia, the longer it takes for strawberries to ripen and the smaller and sweeter they are. Fresh berries make the best caramel, which is served here with mango and orange.

* Mix 2 decilitres of the water with the sugar and boil until the mixture turns golden-brown.
* Hull the strawberries and split the larger ones.
* Add them to the pan, pour on the remaining water and boil for another 5 minutes (the longer it boils, the thicker the caramel).
* Put the caramel aside to cool.

* Stir the ingredients for the toffee crisps until smooth.
* Pour the batter into a piping bag and pipe out five thin sticks at a time, side by side, on a biscuit tray.
* Bake at 175°c for approx. 5 minutes until the sticks have turned an attractive shade of brown.

* Fillet the oranges, i.e. peel them with a sharp knife and cut out the segments. Cut up the mango, and divide the fruit between four bowls. Pour the strawberry caramel on top and garnish with the toffee crisps.

With its many interesting restaurants, Gothenburg challenges Stockholm's claim to be Sweden's gastronomic capital. Jonas Dahlbom to the left.

CARAMEL
3 1/2 dl water
700 g sugar
250 g strawberries

CRISPS
200 g sugar
7 egg whites
125 g flour

SALAD
1 mango
4 oranges

Fillet of roe deer with
polenta, scorzonera and garlic sauce

Here, Nordic venison is combined with both mild and piquant flavours from Mediterranean cuisine. The dish is even more attractive if you slice both the meat and the scorzonera (also known as 'black salsify') lengthwise. The trusty standby of the good Italian cook — polenta — has become the summit of fashion at restaurants around Scandinavia.

MEAT
500–600 g fillet of roe deer
butter for frying
white pepper, freshly ground
salt to taste

POLENTA
1 1/2 dl polenta
9 dl milk
1 artichoke heart
water and lemon juice for
  boiling
10 cm leek, shredded
salt and pepper to taste
butter for frying

SAUCE
3 garlic cloves
1 small onion
6 dl cream
butter for frying
salt and pepper to taste

ACCOMPANIMENT
1 scorzonera root

* Start with the polenta. Simmer the artichoke heart in water with a little lemon juice for approx. 20 minutes, until soft. Mince finely.
* Simmer the polenta grains in milk under a lid for approx. 10 minutes, until the consistency is fairly firm.
* Shred the leek and stir it into the polenta, along with the pieces of artichoke. Season with salt and pepper to taste.
* Turn the polenta out of the pan, shape it into an elongated 'loaf' and leave to cool.
* Cut the polenta into centimetre-thick cubes and brown in butter just before serving.

* Chop the onion and garlic for the sauce and brown them in butter. Add the cream and boil until well thickened.
* Mix the sauce in a blender and season with salt and pepper. To enhance the taste, stir in a little butter before serving.

* Peel, split and cut the scorzonera root into pieces 10–15 centimetres long. Then boil it in lightly salted water until soft.
* Season the roe-deer fillet with salt and pepper and fry in butter to the desired inner temperature. Then set it aside, preferably wrapped in foil, to rest.
* Slice the fillet lengthwise.
* Pour the sauce onto warmed plates, like a mirror, and arrange the fried polenta, fillet and scorzonera attractively on top.

Turbot ragout with
fennel and sun-dried tomatoes

At their best, when grown in the open and ripened in the sun, tomatoes are a superlative cooking ingredient. In the winter and spring, sun-dried tomatoes – often in oil – are often preferable to fresh ones, owing to their more concentrated flavour. Here, the oven-cooked turbot is also accompanied by braised fennel and a small sprig of thyme for added flavour.

* Fillet the turbot and remove the bones and skin. Cut the fish into broad shreds.
* Boil the bones with onion, leek and a root of Hamburg (turnip-rooted) parsley, to make fish stock. Add the white wine and pour on enough water to cover. Simmer for approx. 20 minutes. Strain the stock, of which there should now be approx. 5 decilitres.

* Rinse and trim the fennel bulbs. Cut each into six slices.
* Heat up the olive oil in a sauté pan. Add the garlic, thyme and fennel. Sauté for a minute or so, and then pour the fish stock on top.
* Simmer gently until the liquid is reduced to approx. 2 decilitres. Put in the fish and sun-dried tomatoes. Season with salt and pepper.

* Cook the rice according to the instructions on the pack, but add the vegetables and season with salt. Simmer gently until the rice is cooked. Keep it hot.

* Put the sauté pan in the oven at 175°C (or transfer the ragout to a fireproof dish) just before serving. Stand for approx. 10 minutes. Serve with the freshly boiled rice.

FISH
1.2 kg turbot
salt and pepper

FISH STOCK
bones and discarded parts of
  turbot (see above)
1 onion, in wedges
1/2 leek, sliced
1 root of Hamburg (turnip-
  rooted) parsley, in pieces
1 dl white wine

RAGOUT
3 fennel bulbs
olive oil
1 sprig of thyme
1 garlic clove, finely chopped
1/2 litre fish stock (see above)
25 g butter
700–800 g fillet of turbot
  (see above)
8–12 pieces of sun-dried
  tomatoes

RICE
1 1/2 dl long-grain rice
3 dl water + salt
1/2 onion, finely chopped
1 small carrot, diced
1 piece celeriac, diced

Filleted saddle of lamb
with bulgur and fried garlic

Take a double saddle of lamb and cut the fillets off the bone so that the meat hangs together and can be rolled up with the filling inside. The bones are then used for gravy, which is also flavoured with the juice from the fried garlic.

LAMB
1 1/2 kg saddle of lamb,
    on the bone
1 bunch parsley
1 clove garlic
salt and freshly ground black
    pepper
oil for frying

LAMB GRAVY
lamb bones, hacked to pieces
oil for browning
1 onion, sliced
1/4 celeriac, in pieces
1/2 leek, sliced
2 garlic cloves
1 tbs tomato purée
water
salt and pepper
1 tbs butter

BULGUR
1 1/2 dl bulgur
3 dl chicken stock
1/2 red chili, finely chopped
2 shallots, finely chopped
4 pieces sun-dried tomatoes,
    finely chopped
1 carrot, finely diced
1 tbs butter
salt and freshly ground pepper

GARLIC
25 garlic cloves
water for blanching
2 tbs butter for frying

* Brown the lamb bones in oil and add the vegetables and tomato purée.
* Pour in enough water to cover. Simmer gently for 2–3 hours.
* Strain the stock and reduce it to 2 dl. Season to taste with salt and pepper. Stir a little butter into the gravy just before serving.

* Trim the filleted saddle of lamb. Fill it with finely chopped parsley mixed with pressed garlic, salt and pepper.
* Tie up the meat in a neat roll.
* Brown the meat, turning it in the pan, and then roast it in an oven at 160–175°c for approx. 15 minutes. Put the meat aside for at least as long before carving.

* Sauté the finely chopped chili, shallots, tomatoes and carrots in olive oil.
* Add the bulgur and chicken stock and stir. Simmer gently for 8–9 minutes over gentle heat.

* Stand the mixture beside the cooker until the flavour matures, approx. 10 minutes.
* Season to taste with salt and pepper, and stir in a dab of butter before serving.

* Peel the garlic cloves. Blanch them (i.e. bring them to the boil in new water) 3–4 times to bring out the toothsome, sweet flavour.
* Toss the garlic in butter in a hot pan before serving, and strain the liquid formed into the lamb gravy.

Baked char with coriander apples and vinegar raisins

From the cold tarns, lakes and rivers in north Scandinavia comes the mountain char, a first-class fish. All you really need to bring out the exquisite flavour of this fish — served here with a refreshingly sour apple salad and raisins cooked in sweet vinegar — is a little salt.

* Sprinkle salt on the char fillets. Lay the fish on oven paper with the skin facing up in an oven preheated to 100°c. Leave the fish in the oven until it is thoroughly cooked, approx. 10–15 minutes. Remove the fish and chill.

* Peel two of the apples. Then cut all four apples in wedges and remove the cores.
* Heat up the oil in a saucepan and add the apple wedges with the corian-der seed. Shake the pan now and again. When the apples are soft and hot, season with a little salt to taste.

* Cook the raisins in the vinegar until it is absorbed.

* Lay the fish on the plates, rolling back the skin slightly to reveal the at-tractive flesh. Arrange the apple com-pote beside it and sprinkle the vinegar raisins on top.

Petri Pumpa, in the university town of Lund, has been called 'Sweden's most intelligent restaurant'.

FISH
4 char fillets, with skin
salt

APPLE COMPOTE
4 apples, preferably red and firm
olive oil
1 tbs coriander seeds
salt

ACCOMPANIMENTS
1/2 dl raisins
1/2 dl sweet vinegar

MENU
No. 7

By ERWIN LAUTERBACH
Saison

Tomato terrine with sweet peppers, saffron cream and grilled fish

Apple and Jerusalem artichoke compote

Roast neck of lamb seasoned with dill, lemon and rosemary

Banana and avocado dessert with citrus-fruit salad and fresh berries

RECIPES ON PAGES 130-133

Tomato terrine with sweet peppers, saffron cream and grilled fish

Select very ripe, sweet tomatoes – those slightly past the peak of freshness are good, since their blemished skin often conceals an extra-rich flavour. The terrine should be prepared well ahead, so that it can set properly. Cut it with a thin, sharp knife or (even better) electric knife.

TERRINE
2 red sweet peppers
1 tbs oil
10 tomatoes, well ripened
2 shallots, finely chopped
1 garlic clove, pressed
1 tsp jalapeño (tinned)
3 sheets gelatine (or 1 1/2 tsp gelatine powder)

SAFFRON CREAM
1 1/2 dl whipping cream
juice of 1/4 lemon
8–10 saffron pistils
salt and freshly ground white pepper

ACCOMPANIMENTS
4 fish fillets with skin, e.g. of pike perch, bass or grey mullet
lettuce with fresh herbs

* Cut the stalks off the sweet peppers and remove the seeds. Brush the peppers with oil and bake in the oven at 200°c for approx. 20 minutes until soft and preferably a darkish brown.
* Set the peppers aside to cool slightly. Peel off the skin and chop the flesh finely. Put it in a bowl.
* Dip the tomatoes in boiling water and peel off the skin. Divide the tomatoes into quarters and remove the seeds.
* Chop the shallots and mix them with the jalapeño and garlic. Heat up a little oil in a pan and brown the mixture. Add the tomatoes and sweet peppers, with the juice that has collected in the bowl. Season with salt and pepper, and extra jalapeño if desired (the terrine should be well seasoned).

* Soak the sheets of gelatine (if used) in cold water for 10 minutes. Squeeze out the water and stir the gelatine carefully into the hot tomato mixture until it

melts. Finally, pour the tomato mixture into a ceramic or foil terrine dish that holds approx. 3/4 litre.
* Cover with foil and refrigerate the terrine under light pressure until it has set and can be sliced.

* Boil the cream and saffron for a few minutes. Season with salt, pepper and lemon juice and simmer gently until thickened. Leave to cool.
* To serve, a little extra cream may be needed for the desired consistency.

* Season the fish with salt and pepper, and sauté it gently on the skin side. Do not turn the fish: it then keeps its attractive natural colour on the meat side, and is served on a fried 'bed' of crisp skin.

* Serve a slice of terrine with the grilled fish and saffron cream. Lettuce with fresh herbs is a suitable accompaniment.

Apple and Jerusalem artichoke compote

A small surprise dish before – or halfway through – a meal is always disarming and agreeable for the guest, and a generous, thoughtful gesture on the host's part. This recipe is enough for six or so, depending on the desired portion size.

* Peel the apples, remove the cores and cut up with the artichokes.
* Heat in olive oil without browning, for approx. 3 minutes.
* Season to taste with salt, pepper and lemon juice, and simmer gently under a lid for approx. 15 minutes. Stir now and again to prevent burning.
* Leave to cool. Transfer into open ring moulds on the serving plates, pressing down to make the compote firm.

* Spread salmon roe over the compote and lift away the ring moulds.
* Mix the cream with the lemon juice and stir until the cream thickens. Season with salt and pepper.

* Pour a coil of lemon cream around the compote on each plate, and preferably serve some good white rustic bread as an accompaniment.

Danish 'hygge' (well-being) at Saison.

COMPOTE
2 apples
100 g Jerusalem artichokes, peeled
1 tbs olive oil
salt and pepper to taste
lemon juice

ACCOMPANIMENTS
4–6 tbs salmon roe
1 dl whipping cream
juice of 1/4 lemon

Roast neck of lamb seasoned with dill, lemon and rosemary

When the dill is in bloom, as the crayfish season of the late summer approaches, its scent fills the fields with almost intoxicating strength. The umbels, or flowering heads, provide one of the most distinctive of all Scandinavian seasonings. Here, dill is used as a flavouring for the neck of lamb, which must be roasted in a slow oven for three hours to become truly tender.

* Put the neck of lamb in the oven pan with the seasoning and lemon, and cover with the lid.

* Place the pan (without liquid) in the oven at 150°c and roast the meat slowly for approx. 3 hours.

* Divide the fennel bulbs into halves or quarters. Simmer them gently until soft in lightly salted water. Drain. Before serving, heat the fennel pieces in steam with a little water and a dab of butter.

* Remove the meat, carve out the neck fillets and dish them up on warmed plates.

* Strain the gravy from the lamb into a saucepan, season with salt and pepper if necessary and whisk in a little butter just before serving. Serve the gravy and boiled potatoes separately.

LAMB
1 neck of lamb, approx. 2 kg
salt and pepper
dill umbels (or dill seeds)
1 lemon, sliced
2 sprigs of fresh rosemary

ACCOMPANIMENTS
4 fennel bulbs, boiled
gravy from roasting
1 tbs butter
boiled potatoes

Banana and avocado dessert with citrus-fruit salad and fresh berries

An entirely sugar-free dessert that undoubtedly has a broad appeal. Banana and avocado blend well together, and the fresh tang of citrus fruit is an excellent complement. The dessert should be served ice-cold, almost frozen. Garnish with fresh berries, such as raspberries or wild strawberries.

* Peel the bananas. Mash them lightly with a fork and stir in the juice of one lime.
* Divide the avocado, remove the stone and scoop out the flesh. Mash this with a fork as well, and stir in the juice of the other lime.
* Fill four cups or muffin moulds with equal quantities of mashed banana and avocado. Place in the freezer (if you are in a hurry) or refrigerate overnight. The purée should be ice-cold.

* Cut the oranges and grapefruit into skinless segments.
* Squeeze the juice from the remaining parts of fruit over the segments.
* Empty out the moulds (or cups) like small puddings. Garnish with fresh berries and serve the citrus-fruit salad as an accompaniment.

Saison is a Mecca for gourmets from all over Scandinavia.

FRUIT
2 bananas
1 ripe avocado
2 limes

SALAD
2 oranges
2 grapefruit

Lamb rissoles with squash braised in garlic and potato purée

Growing interest in local raw materials, combined with the strong in-fluence of Mediterranean cuisine, has brought about a renaissance for lamb in Scandinavia. Its characteristic flavour mainly comes from the fat, of which there is some in the mince. The squash (which can be replaced by pumpkin in season) and garlic are Mediterranean touches.

RISSOLES
600 g lamb, coarsely minced
2 1/2 dl single cream
salt
allspice, freshly ground
50 g butter for frying

VEGETABLES
1 whole garlic, in cloves
1 large onion, finely chopped
500 g squash or pumpkin
salt and pepper

POTATO PURÉE
4–5 potatoes
50 g butter
salt and pepper

* Mix the mince with cream and season with coarsely ground allspice and salt. Fry one mini-rissole to sample the taste.
* Shape small, chubby rissoles and fry them gently in butter.

* Peel the pumpkin or squash, and cut the flesh into centimetre-thick pieces.
* Peel the onion and garlic cloves, slice them thinly and cook them gently in a pan with melted butter.
* Add the pumpkin or squash, stir and simmer gently under a lid for 10–15 minutes.
* Season to taste with salt and pepper.

* Peel the potatoes and boil them until soft. Stir them in the saucepan without mashing them completely, add the butter and season to taste with salt and pepper.

David van der Voinstein helps to provide the brisk service at Petri Pumpa in Lund.

OXTAIL
1 1/2 kg oxtail
15 g flour
butter for frying
1 dl red wine
salt and bouquet garni
  (see below)

BOUQUET GARNI
1 garlic clove
sprigs of thyme
bay leaves
black peppercorns

VEGETABLES
1–2 carrots
1/6 celeriac
1 onion
1 root of Hamburg (turnip-
  rooted) parsley
50 g ewe's-milk cheese,
  grated

SAUCE
oxtail gravy (see above)
1 dl red wine
salt and pepper
2 tbs butter

ACCOMPANIMENTS
1 thick leek, blanched
parsley, finely chopped
pressed potatoes

Oxtail in red-wine sauce with vegetables glazed in ewe's-milk cheese

Prolonged stewing of the less desirable animal parts used to be self-evident. Unfortunately, traditional homely fare of this kind is steadily disappearing. Here, red wine and seasonings make oxtail a true delicacy, and it is served elegantly encircled by broad leek leaves.

* Divide the oxtail into pieces at the joints. Cover the pieces of oxtail in flour. Brown the meat in a casserole, pour in the wine, add enough water to cover, salt lightly and insert the bouquet garni.
* Simmer gently under a lid until the oxtail is tender, which takes approx. 1 1/2 hours.
* Clean and trim the vegetables, lay them in the casserole whole and steam them on top of the meat for the last 20 minutes.

* Remove the bouquet garni and vegetables, and transfer them to a bowl. Lift the meat out of the gravy and keep it hot.
* Let the gravy boil until reduced to approx. 2 decilitres. Add the red wine.
* Strain the sauce and season with salt and pepper. Stir in a dab of butter just before the sauce is to be served.

* Pick the meat off the bones and put it back in the bowl.
* Cut the vegetables into even 1-centimetre cubes and mix them with the grated ewe's-milk cheese.

* For the elegant arrangement, use an open, circular mould approx. 7 centimetres in diameter. Press in a portion of meat first, followed by vegetables, and then wrap a broad, blanched leek leaf around the mould. Transfer the mould to a baking tin covered with oven paper. Lift away the mould so that the food is held together by the leek leaf instead. Do the same with the other portions.
* Place the baking tin in an oven preheated to 160°c for approx. 10 minutes before serving.

* Garnish with finely chopped parsley and red-wine sauce, and serve pressed potatoes as a side dish.

Lemon-braised cockerel legs with cabbage in brown sugar

Now and again, splendid cockerels are on sale at the butcher's or in the delicatessen hall. Here, two legs are divided to make a whole meal for four. For more guests the cockerel breasts can, of course, be used as well. The tasty cabbage braised in brown sugar is derived from Danish traditions.

* Divide each leg into two portions – the drumstick and the second joint – to give four equal-sized pieces, each with bones.
* Brown the pieces in oil with finely chopped onion, garlic and diced celeriac.
* After browning the cockerel legs slightly, first pour on lemon juice and cook until it is absorbed. Then add the water, cover and simmer gently for 20–25 minutes.

* Meanwhile, cut the cabbage leaves into triangles and cook them gently until tender in the remaining oil. Sprinkle a little brown sugar on top, cover and stir from time to time.
* Braise the cabbage for 15–20 minutes. Season to taste with salt and pepper from the mill.

* Strain the stock from the cockerel legs, whisk in the butter and season to taste.
* Serve the cockerel legs on a heap of cabbage, surrounded by a little sauce.

Thomas Drejing makes extensive use of organically grown ('Krav'-labelled) raw produce from local suppliers.

COCKEREL
2 cockerel legs, approx.
  600–800 g
1/4 celeriac, diced
1 small onion, finely chopped
2 garlic cloves, chopped
2 tbs olive oil
juice of 1 lemon
2 dl water
2 tbs butter

CABBAGE
500 g white cabbage
2 tbs olive oil
2 tbs brown sugar
salt and pepper

MENU
No. 8

By SEVERIN SJÖSTEDT

Norrlands Bar & Grill

Salt herring with almond-potato salad, Parmesan and browned-butter vinaigrette

Wild-duck breast with pepper gravy, lentils, fungi and confit of duck thighs with herb salad

Bilberry muffins and compote, with vanilla ice cream

RECIPES ON PAGES 142–144

Salt herring with almond-potato salad, Parmesan and browned-butter vinaigrette

Salt herring with potato was once almost the only food on offer to large segments of the Scandinavian population. Today, this old survival fare is eaten mainly on special and festive occasions. Here, the dish is given a more Mediterranean accent, using Parmesan and a balsam vinaigrette.

* Wash the potatoes thoroughly, but leave the peel on.
* Boil the potatoes in salted water. Drain and cut into slices approx. 1/2 centimetre thick.

* Boil the vinegar for the butter vinaigrette until reduced to half.
* Heat the butter until nut-brown and filter through muslin in a sieve, into the vinegar. Press it out of the muslin, using a fork, to extract all the liquid.
* Whisk vigorously, add the lemon rind and season with salt and pepper.

* Mix the potato slices with half the butter vinaigrette and the chives.
* Slice the herring into attractive pieces and dish it up with the potato salad on four plates. Pour the remaining vinaigrette on top of the herring and garnish with red onion, dill and sliced Parmesan.

HERRING
4 fillets of salt herring, drained

POTATO SALAD
10–12 almond potatoes
2 dl balsam vinegar
3 tbs butter, unsalted
1 tsp grated lemon rind
1 tbs chives, finely chopped
salt and pepper to taste

ACCOMPANIMENTS
1 piece of Parmesan
1 bunch of dill
1 red onion

Homage to raw materials on the menu at Norrlands Bar & Grill.

Wild-duck breast with pepper gravy, lentils, fungi and confit of duck thighs with herb salad

This dish is characterised by strong French influences, but the ingredients are entirely Scandinavian. The pepper gravy gives the dish a distinct and potent flavour. To use the whole bird in an appetising way, a confit of duck thighs is served as a side dish.

* Rub the thighs with coarse salt, put them in a dish and chill for 24 hours.
* Then boil the thighs with the bird fat and bouquet garni for approx. 1 hour. The thighs should be very tender but still hold together.
* Grill the thighs in a steak grill so that they take on a decorative pattern, and keep them hot until serving.

* Chop up the carcases and brown the pieces in butter in a casserole. Cut the carrot, onion and leek into pieces, add with the bay leaves and thyme and pour on just enough water to cover.
* Simmer for approx. 3 hours, skimming occasionally.
* Strain the stock and continue reducing until approx. 4 decilitres remain.
* Mix the duck stock in a blender with the white peppercorns and butter. Season with a little salt and strain through a fine sieve. Keep the sauce warm until serving.

* Boil the lentils in the vegetable stock with a little salt for approx. 20 minutes.
* Clean and cut up the fungi, and fry them quickly in butter with the shallots and garlic.
* Mix the fungi with the lentils and keep hot.

* Simmer the scallions in butter without browning.
* Brown the duck breasts on both sides in a frying pan. Bake them until cooked through in a slow oven, 130°c, for approx. 5 minutes.
* Set the breasts aside for a few minutes before slicing them thinly.

* Dish up the mixed fungi and lentils with the scallions on warmed plates, place slices of duck breast on top and pour pepper gravy around the food. Serve the confit of duck thighs with rocket and fresh herbs as a side dish.

DUCK
Breasts, thighs and carcases
  of 2 wild ducks
butter for frying
1 small bouquet garni
1 tbs coarse salt
2 dl duck or goose fat

PEPPER GRAVY
duck carcases (see above)
butter for frying
1 carrot
1 onion
1 leek
1/2 garlic bulb
bay leaves
thyme
1 tbs white peppercorns
1 tbs butter
salt to taste

LENTILS AND FUNGI
1 dl small green lentils
3 dl vegetable stock
200 g fresh
edible fungi (e.g. cèpes,
  chanterelles or oyster fungi)
4 shallots, finely chopped
1 garlic clove, finely chopped
butter for frying

ACCOMPANIMENTS
12 scallions (or spring onions)
butter for frying
rocket
fresh herbs, e.g. chervil,
  tarragon and parsley

Bilberry muffins and compote, with vanilla ice cream

This dessert, based on fairly simple ingredients, rounds off the meal perfectly and presumably appeals to most culinary tastes. Bilberries are the 'universal' berry in Scandinavia: they grow wild in profusion, mainly in the thickly forested central regions. This recipe suffices for six people.

MUFFINS
150 g salted butter
200 g bilberries
500 g sugar
60 g flour
60 g finely ground almonds
7 egg whites

COMPOTE
500 g bilberries
100 g sugar

ICE CREAM
5 dl milk
1 vanilla pod
6 egg yolks
110 g sugar
1 dl whipping cream

ACCOMPANIMENT
rind of 1 lemon

* Sift together the flour, sugar and ground almonds.
* Add the egg whites and whisk until the mixture is well blended.
* Melt the butter over gentle heat until nut-brown, and whisk into the mixture.
* Carefully fold in the bilberries.
* Pour the mixture into a greased muffin pan and bake at 175°c for approx. 20 minutes.

* Boil half the bilberries for the compote with the sugar.
* Strain through a sieve and add the rest of the berries.

* Bring the milk for the ice cream to the boil, with the divided and scraped vanilla pod. Remove the pan from the heat.
* Whisk together the sugar and egg yolks and add the hot vanilla milk, still whisking continuously.

* Simmer until the mixture reaches 70°c, stirring constantly.
* Strain and set aside to cool. Run in an ice-cream machine (or pour into a bowl, put in the freezer and stir now and again until the ice cream is smooth).
* Add the cream at the end, just before the ice cream is ready.

* Serve the bilberry muffins surrounded by the bilberry compote, with a scoop of ice cream on top. Garnish with thin shreds of lemon rind.

The creative elite like to convene at the bar of Norrlands Bar & Grill.

Pineapple with yoghurt ice cream

The leaves from the pineapple are used here as a beautiful decoration, but are not intended for eating. The pineapple itself is 'studded' with vanilla and baked until tender in the oven, in a spicy sauce. A refreshing, low-calorie ice cream is the accompaniment.

* Peel the pineapple. Split the vanilla pods lengthwise, cut them up and 'stud' the pineapple with the vanilla.
* Bring the sauce ingredients to the boil and simmer for approx. 20 minutes. Strain through a fine sieve and pour over the pineapple.
* Place the pineapple in an oven preheated to 190°c for approx. 1 hour. Baste with the sauce about every ten minutes. Cover with foil if the pineapple is becoming too brown.

* Boil the water and 30 g of sugar to make a viscous syrup. Set aside to cool.
* Mix the syrup in a blender with yoghurt (or cottage cheese), cream and the rest (50 g) of the sugar.
* Run the mixture in an ice-cream machine (or pour into a bowl, place it in the freezer and stir from time to time until the ice cream is smooth).

* Slice the pineapple and dish it up on dessert plates.
* Glaze the slices with the sauce, spoon out the ice cream and decorate with a few leaves from the pineapple.

The virtuoso of dessert creation at Bagatelle in Oslo – Jean Guy Borde.

PINEAPPLE
1 fresh pineapple
2 vanilla pods

SAUCE
125 g sugar
1 vanilla pod
5 thin slices of fresh ginger
1/2 chili, finely chopped
1 banana, mashed
1 tbs dark rum

ICE CREAM
3 tbs water
30 + 50 g sugar
250 g yoghurt (or cottage cheese)
1/2 dl whipping cream

Budapest roll with raspberry cream and chocolate sauce

ROLL
165 g egg whites (about 5–6,
  depending on size)
3 dl sugar
150 g hazelnuts
1 dl flour
1 1/2 tbs cocoa

CREAM
175 g raspberries
25 g sugar (or frozen,
  sweetened raspberries)
1 sheet gelatine (or 1/2 tsp
  gelatine powder)
15 g golden syrup
3 dl whipping cream

DARK CHOCOLATE SAUCE
1 dl cocoa
1 dl sugar
1 dl water

WHITE CHOCOLATE SAUCE
200 g white chocolate,
  in pieces
1 dl cream

ACCOMPANIMENTS
chocolate sticks or similar for
  decorating

Two kinds of chocolate sauce – one dark and one white – and cream flavoured with raspberry sauce make this dessert a dream for the sweet-toothed. Two chocolate sticks resembling antennae make a striking garnish, but chocolate in other shapes and forms serve just as well.

∗ Beat the egg whites with the sugar.
∗ Finely chop the nuts and mix with flour and cocoa. Fold into the egg-white mixture.
∗ Butter a baking sheet or cover it with oven paper, and spread out the mixture. Bake at 175°c for approx. 7 minutes.
∗ Remove the sheet from the oven and let it cool slightly. Cut out pieces measuring 15 x 7 centimetres, and shape into cylinders while the cake is still warm. Leave to cool.

∗ Blend the raspberries with the sugar, and strain.
∗ Mix approx. 25 g of the raspberry purée with the gelatine and syrup, and melt in a saucepan over gentle heat.
∗ Add the rest of the raspberry purée and chill thoroughly.
∗ Whip the cream and mix it with the cold raspberry sauce, but save a little sauce for serving.

∗ Mix the ingredients for the dark chocolate sauce and simmer while stirring for approx. 10 minutes.
∗ Strain before serving.

∗ Bring to the boil the cream for the white chocolate sauce.
∗ Take the pan off the heat, add the white chocolate and let it melt into the cream. Mix thoroughly.

∗ Stand the Budapest rolls on end and pipe the raspberry cream inside the cylinders.
∗ Pour a little dark chocolate sauce on top of the cream. Decorate the plates with raspberry sauce and the dark and white chocolate sauce. The composition is especially stylish with chocolate in some attractive shape, e.g. sticks.

Fig tart with custard cream and red-wine caramel

This dessert is a perfect one to prepare well in advance. Both the custard cream and the sauce that are served with it are, of course, suitable accompaniments for many other desserts.

PASTRY
125 g unsalted butter, at room temperature
90 g sugar
1 egg
250 g wheat flour
1/4 tsp salt

CUSTARD
3 dl milk
1 vanilla pod, split and scraped
50 g sugar
3 egg yolks
45 g flour
1 tbs cornflour

FIGS
8 fresh figs
1/2 dl icing sugar

RED-WINE CARAMEL
3 dl good red wine
75 g sugar

ACCOMPANIMENTS
2 tbs custard (see above)
2 dl cream

* Start with the pastry dough. Blend the sugar and butter until smooth.
* Add the egg and briefly run the blender again.
* Sift together the salt and flour, scrape the dough from the sides of the blender and add the dry ingredients gradually, with the blender at low speed. Turn the blender off as soon as the dough starts to stick together.
* Knead the dough by hand, wrap it in plastic foil and chill in the refrigerator for at least one hour.
* Roll out the dough until it is approx. 1 1/5–2 mm thick. Line four small tart pans or one large one with the dough, letting a little hang over the side. Cover with foil and chill for approx. 20 minutes.
* Take out the tart pan(s) and fill with, for example, dried yellow peas as a weight on top of the foil. Bake in the oven at 175°c for 10–12 minutes.
* Lift away the foil and peas, and trim off the pastry that is hanging over the side(s). Cool.

* Beat the egg yolks for the custard with the sugar and add the cornflour.
* Boil the milk with the vanilla and pour into the mixture. Beat continuously.
* Simmer the custard, stirring constantly, until thickened.
* Pour the custard into a mixing bowl, cover with plastic foil and cool.

* Slice the figs thinly and lay them on a baking sheet. Powder with icing sugar and glaze at 200°c for approx. 4–6 minutes, until the sugar has melted.

* Boil the wine and sugar together until caramelised, approx. 5–10 minutes.

* Fill the tart(s) with custard, but save approx. 2 tbs for serving. Distribute the figs attractively on top.
* Whip the cream lightly and stir in the remaining custard.
* Serve the fig tart surrounded by caramel sauce and custard cream.

Apple charlotte with cardamom and crème fraîche

This is a miniature work of art in its own right, with the tangy apple purée surrounded by the band of oven-baked, gauze-thin slices of apple. It is at its very best when made of sour Siberian crab apples, picked when the brief Scandinavian summer gives way to autumn.

* Cook an apple purée out of the apples and white wine. Add the sugar, cardamom, flour, vanilla scrapings and egg yolks.
* Pour the mixture into a small saucepan and simmer gently, stirring constantly.
* Soak the sheets of gelatine (if used) in water for 10 minutes, and then squeeze out the water. Stir the gelatine into the hot apple purée until melted. Set the purée aside to cool.
* Whip the cream and stir it into the apple purée. Fill four aluminium portion moulds (the disposable kind), and refrigerate them for 24 hours or so.

* Make a thin apple jelly for the sauce, using the red apple peel. Cover the peel with water and simmer for 30 minutes. Strain off the juice and continue boiling it with the sugar. When the sauce begins to thicken, it is ready.

* Divide the two apples for the outer covering. Remove the cores and slice the apples very thinly. Lay them, overlapping like roof tiles, in four straight rows on the oven paper. Each row of apple should be long enough to go round one apple charlotte.
* Transfer to a baking tin, brush with melted butter and sprinkle with a little sugar.
* Put the baking tin in the oven at 150°C for 10–12 minutes. Leave to cool on the baking tin.

* Detach the apple purée from the moulds and lay it on the rows of apple slices. Roll up each charlotte so that the two ends of the row of apples overlap slightly. Shape each charlotte into a 'ball', and dish up on four dessert plates.

* Serve with a dollop of whipped cream on top, a little red apple-jelly sauce around it and a few whole cardamom seeds as decoration on the plates.

FILLING
125 g crab apples, peeled and cored
1/2 dl white wine
20 g sugar
1/4 tsp cardamom
1/4 tbs flour
1/4 vanilla pod, scraped out
2 egg yolks
2 sheets gelatine (or 1 tsp gelatine powder)
1 1/2 dl whipping cream

APPLE CASE
2 firm apples (Golden Delicious)
1 tbs melted butter
1 tbs sugar

JELLY SAUCE
red peel and cores of the crab apples
sugar + water

ACCOMPANIMENTS
1 dl whipping cream
whole cardamom seeds

Cloudberry cake with vanilla sauce

Cloudberries grow wild in the wetlands of northern Scandinavia. The berries are replete with vitamin C and have a refreshing, tangy flavour that resembles nothing else. The 'preserve' used here consists simply of freshly picked, raw cloudberries packed in a wooden barrel or other container; no additive is required, since the berries contain their own preservative. The cake provides 8–10 portions.

CAKE
100 g almond paste
100 g butter or margarine
2 eggs
100 g sugar
1 heaped tbs wheat flour

FILLING
2 dl apricot jam
1 tbs Lakka liqueur (optional)
2 dl cloudberry preserve +
  2 tbs sugar

VANILLA CUSTARD
3 dl single cream
1 small vanilla pod
3 egg yolks
2 tbs sugar
2 dl whipping cream

* Mix the almond paste with the butter or margarine, eggs, sugar and wheat flour.
* Lay a sheet of oven paper on a baking tin and spread out the mixture on the paper. Bake in the oven at 175–180°C for approx. 10 minutes or until the mixture has turned golden brown.
* Turn out the cake on a lightly sugared pastry board. Leave to cool slightly. Cut the cake horizontally into two equal halves.

* Mix the apricot jam with liqueur or water to give a spreading consistency.
* Spread the jam over one half of the cake. Put the other half on top, light side up.
* Sweeten the cloudberry preserve with sugar to taste.
* Cover the cake with preserve and chill until serving.

* Divide the vanilla pod and scrape out its contents into the single cream in a saucepan. Add the pod and bring to the boil.
* Remove the pan from the heat and set aside to cool. Take out the pieces of vanilla pod.
* Beat the egg yolks and sugar, and pour the mixture into the cream.
* Simmer gently, whisking continuously, until the sauce is fairly thick. Take care not to let it boil, or it will separate.
* Leave the sauce to cool. Whip the cream och fold it into the sauce before serving.

* Trim the sides of the cake and divide it into portions.
* Serve the cake with vanilla sauce on one side.

Apples and pears in elderflower juice with almond-rice sauce

When the elder trees are in bloom, giving off their distinctive, almost overpowering scent, we Scandinavians know that summer has begun. We use both the flowers and the berries to flavour desserts, fruit squashes and aperitifs. This elderflower dessert, with apples and pears, is a glorious colour and utterly delicious. The sauce, made of Italian avorio rice, is an ingenious and versatile concoction.

∗ Peel the fruit. Simmer it gently, covered, in elderflower juice perhaps diluted with water (depending how concentrated it is) until soft. Turn the fruit from time to time during the cooking, and keep an eye on them to make sure they do not become overcooked and fall apart. The cooking time depends on the kind of fruit used.

∗ Let the fruit cool in the juice. Pour the juice over the fruit from time to time to prevent it from drying out.

∗ Remove some of the juice, add a little more sugar and boil until the juice has thickened to an almost syrupy viscosity. This can be done in advance.

∗ Blanch, peel and sauté the almonds in a little butter in a saucepan. Leave on the heat for approx. 5 minutes.

∗ Add the rice, pour on the milk and scrape the inside of a vanilla pod into the pan. Simmer gently until all the liquid is gone.

∗ Pick out the almonds and put them aside for the time being. Process the rice quickly in the blender until it is a smooth, but fairly thick purée. Place the purée in the freezer.

∗ When the purée is half-frozen, process it in the blender again, diluting with a little milk if it is too thick. The sauce should now be viscous and airy.

∗ Rinse the almonds, dry them and brown them in a pan with a little sugar and a few drops of water until caramelised.

∗ Serve the fruit with the thickened elderflower juice and the freshly blended, ice-cold almond-rice sauce.

FRUIT
1 litre elderflower juice,
  containing berries
4 pears and/or apples

SAUCE
1 dl avorio (arborio) rice
3–4 dl milk
1 vanilla pod
30 sweet almonds, blanched
  and peeled
2 tbs butter

Pale chocolate mousse with
vinegar sultanas and finger biscuits

The tangy sultanas that accompany this chocolate mousse should be cooked the day before, and left to swell in the vinegar syrup overnight. The biscuits can also be prepared in advance. The mousse itself, on the other hand, is at its very best when freshly made and just below room temperature.

SULTANAS
1 1/2 dl sultanas
3 tbs sugar
1/2 dl sherry vinegar
1 dl water

BISCUITS
4 eggs
1 1/2 dl sugar (or slightly less)
2 1/2 dl flour

MOUSSE
125 g milk chocolate (Calebaut or similar)
1 1/2 dl whipping cream
3 egg yolks
3 tbs sugar
15 g butter

* Cook the sultanas in water and vinegar, with the sugar, for approx. 5 minutes. Stand for 24 hours or so before serving.

* Beat the eggs and sugar for the biscuits until the mixture is porous, and then gently fold in the flour with a plastic or rubber scraper.
* Pipe the mixture out in 'fingers' on a baking tin covered with oven paper. Bake in the oven at 175°c until they are crisp and an attractive golden brown.

* Melt the chocolate with the butter in a bain-marie.
* Whip the cream until frothy.
* Beat the egg yolks with the sugar over a gentle heat (preferably in a bain-marie) until the mixture has reached 70°c.
* Mix the melted chocolate with the beaten egg yolks, and leave to cool.

When the chocolate mixture has cooled to 25°c, fold in the whipped cream.
* Put in a cool place, but not in the refrigerator, until the chocolate mousse is to be served.
* Serve the mousse surrounded by the biscuits and sultanas.

'Less is more' is not part of Bo Jacobsen's creed.

Pumpkin compote
with orange in ginger foam

This compote derives an extra good flavour from candied orange peel. The peel must be cooked well ahead, but can be stored in large quantities and kept as a standby in the larder. Pumpkins also keep for long periods and, moreover, are available in many different decorative varieties.

ORANGES
peel of 1/2 orange
1 dl water
1 dl sugar

COMPOTE
400 g pumpkin
1 orange, filleted segments
1 dl orange juice
1 dl sugar
1/2 tsp grated fresh ginger
candied orange peel (see
  above)

GINGER FOAM
3 egg yolks
1 tbs sugar
1 1/2 dl white wine
1 tsp fresh grated ginger

* Pare off the outermost layer of orange peel. Lay it in a saucepan with the water and sugar.
* Cover and leave for approx. 3 hours over minimum heat, without boiling.
* Refrigerate the orange peel overnight (at least 6 hours).

* Divide the pumpkin into small pieces. Place in a saucepan, pour in the orange juice and add the sugar and ginger. Boil to make a compote.
* Strain the juice and boil until thickened.
* Fillet one orange, i.e. peel it with a knife and remove all the white pith. Then cut out skinless wedges with a thin, sharp knife.
* Mix the compote with the filleted orange and finely chopped, candied orange peel.
* Chill the compote.

* For the ginger foam, whisk the sugar, eggs and wine over gentle heat until a stiff foam is formed.
* Add ginger to taste, and serve with the chilled compote.
* Garnish the dessert with orange wafers.

Pears filled with almond paste and aniseed sauce

In Scandinavia, almost every private garden has a few fruit trees — cherries, plums, apples or pears — on its southern side. The fruit ripens relatively slowly, but the flavours are concentrated and excellent. And, of course, there is no fruit that tastes as good as the home-grown kind.

* Peel the pears. Remove the cores from beneath with a corer in such a way that the whole pear retains its shape.
* Boil the water and sugar.
* Wedge the pears into a saucepan as tightly as possible. Pour on the syrup and simmer the pears gently until they are just soft.
* Leave the pears to cool in the syrup.

* Beat the almond paste until smooth with the liqueur (or water).
* Remove the pears from the syrup. After draining, fill them with almond paste.

* Simmer the cream gently with the sugar, cinnamon and star aniseed for approx. 5 minutes.
* Extract the seasonings and remove the pan from the heat.
* Beat together the egg and egg yolk with a couple of tablespoonfuls of cream.

* Pour the egg mixture into the hot cream, place the saucepan over gentle heat and whisk until the sauce thickens. NB take care not to let it boil, or it will separate.
* Stand the saucepan in cold water and whisk until the sauce is cold.

* Serve the pears with the sauce and garnish with a sprig of fresh mint.

PEARS
4 ripe pears
5 dl water + 1 1/2 dl sugar

FILLING
80–100 g almond paste
1–2 tbs apricot liqueur
(or water)

SAUCE
2 dl whipping cream
1/2 dl sugar
1 egg + 1 egg yolk
4 whole star aniseed
1 stick of cinnamon

ACCOMPANIMENT
sprigs of mint

Apple in rosemary butterscotch sauce

Scandinavian apples have a highly distinctive flavour of concentrated acidity and sweetness, the effect of slow maturation in a cool climate. They are harvested before the first frost, when the air is clear and the sun still has some warmth. If the apples are unblemished and attractive in colour, the peel should be left on. Otherwise, the apples should be peeled before they are cut into wedges.

* Brown the sugar in a saucepan.
* Pour in the cream and boil to make a thin butterscotch sauce.
* Add the rosemary.
* Cut the apples in wedges and remove the cores.

* Lay the pieces of apple in the hot butterscotch sauce and stir to mix thoroughly.
* Lay a sheet of filo pastry on oven paper on a baking tray. Brush with melted butter, place small sprigs of rosemary on top and cover with another sheet of filo pastry. Place oven paper and a light weight on top.
* Bake in the oven at 150–175°c for approx. 20 minutes. Set aside to cool.
* Break the filo pastry into attractive pieces and decorate the compote as in the picture.

Thomas Drejing's culinary art is entirely based on regional products.

APPLE BUTTERSCOTCH
3 large, firm and sourish
   apples
1/2 dl sugar
1 dl whipping cream
1 tsp chopped rosemary

WAFER
4 small sprigs of rosemary
2 sheets filo pastry (available
   ready-made)

[Metric – UK/US]

CAPACITY

1 tablespoon = 1 tablespoon

1 teaspoon = 1 teaspoon

1 milliliter – 1/5 teaspoon

5 milliliters – 1 teaspoon

15 milliliters = 1 tablespoon

1 deciliter = 0.36 UK cups = 3.6 UK fluid oz. = 7 tsp.

1 deciliter = 0.42 US cups = 3.4 US fluid oz. = 7 tsp.

2.8 deciliters = 1 UK cup = 10 UK fluid oz. = 20 tsp.

2.4 deciliters = 1 US cup = 8 US fluid oz. = 16 tsp.

1 liter = 1.75 UK pints

1 liter = 2.1 US pints

1 liter = 0.88 UK liquid quarts

1 liter = 1.06 US liquid quarts

WEIGHT

1 gram = .035 oz.

100 grams = 3.5 oz.

500 grams = 1.10 pounds

1 kilogram = 2.205 pounds

1 kilogram = 35 oz.

TEMPERATURES

$0°$ Celsius = $32°$ Farenheit

$50°$ C = $120°$ F

$75°$ C = $165°$ F

$100°$ C = $210°$ F

$125°$ C = $255°$ F

$150°$ C = $300°$ F

$175°$ C = $350°$ F

$200°$ C = $390°$ F

$225°$ C = $435°$ F

$250°$ C = $480°$ F

$275°$ C = $525°$ F

$300°$ C = $570°$ F

$325°$ C = $615°$ F

$350°$ C = $660°$ F

To convert Celsius to Farenheit multiply by 9, divide by 5 and add 32.

ENGLISH, *dansk, norsk, svenska*

ALLSPICE, *allehånde, allehånde, kryddpeppar*
ALMOND, *mandel, mandel, mandel*
ALMOND PASTE, *mandelmasse, mandelmasse, mandelmassa*
ANCHOVY, *ansjos, ansjos, sardell*
ANISEED, *anis, anis, anis*
ARTICHOKE, GLOBE, *artiskok, artiskokk, kronärtsskocka*
ARTICHOKE, JERUSALEM, *jordskok, jordskokk, jordärtsskocka*
BASIL, *basilikum, basilikum, basilika*
BASS, *havaborre, havabbor, havsabborre*
BAY LEAF, *laurbærblad, laurbærblad, lagerblad*
BEEF MARROW, *marv, marg, märg*
BEETROOT, *rødbede, rødbete, rödbeta*
BILBERRY, *blåbær, blåbær, blåbär*
CABBAGE, *hvidkål, hodekål, vitkål*
CARAWAY, *kommen, karve, kummin*
CARDAMOM, *kardemomme, kardemomme, kardemumma*
CARROT, *gulerod, gulrot, morot*
CELERIAC, *knoldselleri, sellerirot, rotselleri*
CELERY, *bladselleri, stangselleri, blekselleri*
CÈPES, *karl-johansvamp, stensopp, karl johansvamp*
CHANTERELLE, *kantarel, kantarell, kantarell*
CHAR, *fjeldørred, røye, röding*
CHERVIL, *kørvel, kjørvel, körvel*
CHICKEN, *kylling, kylling, kyckling*
CHICORY, *julesalat, sikori, endive*
CHIVES, *purløg, gressløk, gräslök*
CLOUDBERRY, *multebær, multer, hjortron*
CLOVES, *kryddernelliker, nellik, kryddnejlika*
COCKEREL, *hanekylling, hanekylling, tupp*
COD, *torsk, torsk, torsk*
CORIANDER, *koriander, koriander, koriander*
COS LETTUCE, *romersk salat, romanosalat, romansallad*
COURGETTE, *courgette, zucchini, zucchini*
CRAB, *krabbe, krabbe, krabba*
CRANBERRY, *tranebær, tranebær, tranbär*
CRAYFISH, *krebs, kreps, kräfta*
CUCUMBER, *agurk, agurk, gurka*
DILL, *dild, dill, dill*
DUCK, *and, and, anka*
EEL, *ål, ål, ål*
ELDER, *hyld, hyll, fläder*
FALLOW DEER, *dådyr, dådyr, dovhjort*
FENNEL, *fennikel, fennikel, fänkål*
FIG, *figen, fiken, fikon*
FLOUR, *mel, mel, mjöl*
GARLIC, *hvidløg, hvitløk, vitlök*

GINGER, *ingefær, ingefær, ingefära*
GREY MULLET, *multe, mulle, multe*
HALIBUT, *helleflynder, kveite/hellefisk, hälleflundra*
HAMBURG PARSLEY, *persillerod, persillerot, persiljerot*
HERRING, *sild, sild, sill*
HORSERADISH, *peberrod, pepperrot, pepparrot*
LAMB, *lam, lam, lamm*
LEEK, *porre, purreløk, purjolök*
LENTILS, *linser, linser, linser*
LETTUCE, *salat, salat, sallad*
LINGONBERRY, *tyttebær, tyttebær, lingon*
LOBSTER, *hummer, hummer, hummer*
MANGE-TOUT, *sukkerærter, sukkererter, sockerärter*
MORELS, *morkler, morkler, murklor*
MUSHROOM, *champignon, champignon, champinjon*
OCEAN PERCH, *rødfisk, uer, uer*
ONION, *løg, løk, lök*
ORANGE, *appelsin, appelsin, apelsin*
OYSTER, *østers, østers, ostron*
PARSLEY, *persille, persille, persilja*
PEAR, *pære, pære, päron*
PIKE PERCH, *sandart, gjørs, gös*
PORK, *svinekød/flæsk, gris/flesk, gris/fläsk*
PUMPKIN, *græskar, gresskar, pumpa*
QUAIL, *vagtel, vaktel, vaktel*
RADISH, *radise, reddik, rädisor*
RAISINS, *rosiner, rosin, russin*
RASPBERRY, *hindbær, bringebær, hallon*
ROCKET, *salatsennep, rucolasalat, ruccolasallad*
ROE DEER, *rådyr, rådyr, rådjur*
ROSEMARY, *rosmarin, rosmarin, rosmarin*
SAFFRON, *safran, safran, saffran*
SALMON, *laks, laks, lax*
SCALLOP, *kammusling, kamskjell, pilgrimsmussla*
SCAMPI, *scampi, sjøkreps, havskräfta*
SCORZONERA ROOT, *skorzonerrod, skorsonnerrot, svartrot*
SHALLOT, *chalotteløg, sjalottløk, schalottenlök*
SPINACH, *spinat, spinat, spenat*
SWEDE, *kålrod, kålrot, kålrot*
SWEET PEPPER, *paprika, paprika, paprika*
TARRAGON, *estragon, estragon, dragon*
THYME, *timian, timian, timjan*
TUNA, *tun, tunfisk, tonfisk*
TURBOT, *pighvar, pigghvar, piggvar*
VEAL, *kalv, kalv, kalv*
VENISON, *hjort, hjort, hjort*
WALNUT, *valnød, valnøtt, valnöt*
WITCH/POLE FLOUNDER, *rødtunge, smørflyndre, rödtunga*